AF544927

481
483
Rio Grande

AMERICAN NARROW GAUGE

John Krause

with

Donald Duke

Golden West Books

· San Marino, California ·

AMERICAN NARROW GAUGE

Published by Golden West Books
San Marino, California 91108 U.S.A.
Library of Congress Catalog Card No. 78-12544
I.S.B.N. 0-87095-059-2

Library of Congress Cataloging in Publication Data

Krause, John.
American narrow gauge.

Bibliography: p.
Includes index.
1. Railroads, Narrow-gage—United States—History.
I. Duke, Donald, 1929- joint author. II. Title.
TF23.K74 385'.5'0973 78-12544

ACKNOWLEDGEMENTS

During the five years the *American Narrow Gauge* has been in process, many friends have come to my rescue. For the picture material contributed to this book, either of their own photographic artistry or from collections of which they are owners or custodians, I am in debt to the following: Robert B. Adams, Gary Allen, Lucius Beebe, Murray Befeler, Gerald M. Best, Kent W. Cochrane, Richard J. Cook, Donald Duke, Denis Dunning, Guy L. Dunscomb, Mallory Hope Ferrell, Phil Hastings, Cornelius W. Hauck, Henry R. Griffiths, Jr., R. B. Jackson, D. Wallace Johnson, R. H. Kindig, Otto Perry, H. Reid, Robert W. Richardson, Phil Ronfor, Jim Shaughnessy, Dick Steinheimer, and August Thieme.

I wish to thank Karl Hesper of Photo Communications for his careful execution of the lithographic camera while making the fine halftones in this volume. Also to Debbie Dunn for the scaling and drawing of the railroad maps.

Appreciation is extended to Donald Duke for his fine research and preparation of the text material and the writing of the captions accompanying the illustrations. Special mention must be given to Robert W. Richardson of the Colorado Railroad Museum for his research time and checking the text and captions for accuracy.

Finally, I would like to acknowledge the encouragement and support of Golden West Books for their faith in this book project.

TITLE PAGE ILLUSTRATION

Although narrow-gauge operations in the United States were widespread and reached from Maine to the Blue Mountains of Oregon and from Michigan to the Owens Valley in California, nowhere did they lend so special a character to the landscape than on Marshall Pass in Colorado. In the title page illustration, locomotives Nos. 481 and 483 easily handle a tonnage freight up the four percent grade on the west side of Marshall Pass. — WATERCOLOR BY HOWARD FOGG — COURTESY OF THOMAS B. MOORE.

Golden West Books

A Division of Pacific Railroad Publications, Inc.

P.O. BOX 8136 • SAN MARINO, CALIFORNIA • 91108

Preface

I first came in contact with John Krause way back in the late 1940's while attending Colorado College located in Colorado Springs. Naturally I chose Colorado to go to school as it was near the Denver & Rio Grande Western narrow-gauge lines. During one of the school holidays I decided to drive down to Alamosa and do a bit of narrow-gauge photography. I had phoned Bob Richardson, proprietor of the *Narrow Gauge Motel,* in advance to reserve a room and learn if there would be any rail activity during the week. The motel was a good operating base and the Alamosa-Durango main line passed right in front of the motel. Richardson was always well informed on train operations and also knew how to reach the best photographic spots on both the Denver & Rio Grande and Rio Grande Southern lines.

Skipped an afternoon laboratory class so I could leave a bit earlier for Alamosa. I wanted to have dinner with Bob and attempt to get to bed early. That was not always possible as Bob liked to talk narrow-gauge way into the morning if he could find someone with a good ear. A Chama bound freight was scheduled to leave Alamosa shortly after the daily passenger train *San Juan.* If things worked out right, one could follow the *San Juan* to Antonito, double back and catch the freight and follow it to Lava Tank. Due to the lack of any roads in narrow-gauge country it was pretty hard to catch it again until it reached Los Pinos loop below Cumbres station late in the afternoon. Anyway that was my program for the day.

The sun was beginning to dip in the West as I drove down U.S. 285 south of Alamosa on the road to Santa Fe, New Mexico. As I pulled into the motel there was Bob Richardson out turning on the "No Vacancy" sign. I gave a honk and he climbed into the front seat and we headed for the office. Alongside one of the motel rooms I spotted a tan-colored Ford with New York license plates and a huge Baldwin Locomotive Works engine number plate mounted on the front. The usual canvas water bags were hanging from the front bumper. Naturally, I put on the brakes for a closer look and then turned to Richardson. "What the hell is that?" I asked with a puzzled look on my face. "Some new kind of Rio Grande Southern *Galloping Goose?"*

"Nope," Richardson replied. "Didn't think you would spot it that quick, though. That hunk of tin belongs to a guy named Krause from New York, and he's even a nuttier narrow-gauge buff than you guys from California." He went on to say, "You think that car is something, well you should see the gadget he has to mount two Speed Graphic cameras on so he can take two shots at one time." While I was signing the register, Richardson showed me some of Krause's photographic work. I must say I was impressed and some of his action shots were fantastic. Bob informed me that he took that car of his into those obscure and remote spots.

After getting settled in the room I went back to

the office to get Bob so we could head for the only decent cafe in Alamosa. Ptomaine Tommys was the only place one dared eat if you wanted to be mobile the next day, as Alamosa was lacking in gourmet restaurants. On the way to the car we stopped at Krause's door to see if he wanted to join us for dinner. Richardson knocked on the door and he spoke out as it opened a crack, "We're going downtown for dinner, want to come along?" Food must have sounded good to Krause as the door was flung open and I had my first meeting with the great John Krause. We have been friends since that time.

Naturally, we spent part of the week together photographing and chasin' trains. Over the years we met at Durango or Silverton a time or two to do a bit more photographing. We have corresponded, traded pictures, and generally kept in touch. After I started Golden West Books I talked John into putting together *Rails Through Dixie,* a pictorial history of railroads down South, especially the rust stained Shay geared locomotives and creaky tea-kettle engines in remote reaches of Arkansas and the Carolinas.

Some years ago I suggested to Krause he should put his narrow-gauge act together as he had some great "stuff" on the Denver & Rio Grande Western lines. At the time the market was loaded with books about the D&RG narrow-gauge, and while most of them were just pictures and captions, they had pretty well captured the market. After putting heads together, some additional planning and organization, it was decided we should expand the project and produce a book featuring the narrow-gauge lines of the nation following World War II.

John and I had pretty well photographed the current scene in Colorado, he had captured on film the East Broad Top and East Tennessee & Western North Carolina, and I had been to the Southern Pacific narrow-gauge any number of times. The West Side Lumber Co. with their Shay geared engines had just quit and I had photographed that from one end to the other. It was decided we should produce the *American Narrow-Gauge.* There were a few lines still operating and most of the enthusiasts had read about them in *Trains* or *Railroad Magazine.*

Negatives and prints were passed back and forth. What we did not have, such friends as Phil Hastings, Phil Ronfor, Bob Richardson, Dick Kindig, and Dick Steinheimer, to name a few, filled in. H. Reid came to the rescue on some of the obscure lines down South and volunteered to coordinate the text. John Hungerford agreed to write about the East Broad Top which was a favorite of his at the time, and I felt I could work something out on the other lines. Everything appeared to be in order and *American Narrow-Gauge* would be in print in a year or two.

First off Reid got sick and a couple of years rolled around with no basic text to go along with the illustrations. John Hungerford then passed away without writing a line about the East Broad Top. All I had at the time were notes, but I was over confident that a text could be put together in short order. That was a big mistake, to say the least. After preparing the layout design for this volume last fall I began to sink my teeth into the various books which would provide the material required to introduce narrow-gauge to the reader, and a little introductory material about each of the lines presented in the photographs. This seemed simple enough, but the more I read the less I knew about narrow-gauge. When I asked questions of railroad experts I got this response, "Well — ah, yes — narrow-guage, it's three-feet between the tracks and the engines and rolling stock are smaller than standard gauge. There are lines in Colorado and Pennsylvania, and the Southern Pacific has a narrow-gauge branch in the Owens Valley of California." I knew all that, but what I did not know was "Why did they build narrow-gauge in the first place when the nation had already set a standard of four feet, eight and one-half inches between rails?" Also I wondered, "Why did they develop outside frames and what road had them first?" These are just two of many questions that went unanswered for a long time and why this book has been late in its arrival to your bookshelf.

Krause was rightfully becoming impatient. *American Narrow-Gauge* had been derailed too many times. I was beginning to wonder myself if this project would ever be finished. As a publisher, I was of the opinion that this book should tell a story. Trade journals were read, books digested, and searching phone calls made to narrow-gauge authority Richardson, curator of the Colorado Railroad Museum at Golden, Colorado. At long last things began to fall in place. The end was in sight.

Considering that narrow-gauge railroads around-the-world provided less than five percent of the world's railroad mileage, we can thank someone upstairs for allowing the American narrow-gauge lines to linger as long as they did. I am pleased I am old enough to have seen the little trains, to ride the "Galloping Goose" and to have had the fun in taking a few of these photographs. John and I hope that *American Narrow-Gauge* brings the reader as much pleasure as we had putting it all together.

August 1978

Donald Duke - Publisher
Golden West Books

Introduction

No chapter in the colorful saga of American railroading is so heavily freighted with nostalgia as the age of the narrow-gauge. As subject matter, the topic is glamourous, quaint, and endearing. An unsuspecting reader might conclude that narrow-gauge was a most significant occurrence in railroad history, and the utopia on this earth was the western region of Colorado with its famous narrow-gauge lines.

American Narrow-Gauge is not a detailed and technical history about the nation's narrow-gauge lines constructed since 1871, but basically a luxurious pictorial account of narrow-gauge lines still in operation following World War II. To fully comprehend what narrow-gauge is all about and how impractical it was in a nation with an established standard gauge, it is necessary to present a bit of background history about the narrow-gauge principle.

At the close of the Civil War in 1865, America once again turned to building a transcontinental railroad and to settling and developing the vast lands west of the Mississippi River. The migration to the West was accelerated by the discovery of gold in California in 1849 and demonstrated the urgent need for better forms of transportation. Delayed by the war, an era began which typified all of the courage, ingenuity and perseverance that is part of the American legend. This was the age of steam and the opening of the American West.

The railroad had played a great part in the Civil War, but it was quickly learned that various track gauges were impractical. There were no fewer than 23 gauges in use at the time, ranging from two-foot to six-foot in the country. This resulted in the narrowing of all "broad-gauge" track to a set standard of four feet eight and one-half inches between rails during 1866 to 1883. Many of the smaller gauges were tram roads used in industrial lines. With the adoption of standard gauge, cars could be interchanged from one line to another, thus avoiding the costly transfer of loads.

During the early history of railways in England, a great controversy arose among engineers as to the best gauge to be adopted. Two eminent engineers, the greatest of the time, I.K. Brunel and George Stephenson, took opposite sides, and divided the profession into two hostile camps. The controversy lasted 20 years and every argument that skill and ingenuity could invent was brought into play. Finally Stephenson's gauge was selected as the result of an accident. It seems that when the parts of the first locomotive were being put together, it was found to fit a gauge of four feet eight and one-half inches, instead of four feet nine inches as was intended. With few exceptions this gauge was established as standard throughout the world.

The initial narrow-gauge railway, the Festiniog of North Wales, was originally constructed as an industrial line in 1832 and operated as a horse drawn tramway to carry slate from the quarries. A gauge of two feet was selected for economy as well as stability. Two four-wheel steam locomotives were built for the line in 1863 by G. England & Co. with a weight of eight tons per engine. Subsequently five other engines were built, two of them being heavier, and weighing ten tons in working order. The year 1869 was marked by the introduction of the Fairlie engine on the Festiniog Railway and proved this double-ended type engine practical on narrow-gauge lines.

During the 1860's a second frontier was developing in the American West, that of the Rocky Mountain miner and prospector. The craze for a cheaper form of rail transport was developing. General William J. Palmer, fresh from the Civil War, assisted in the construction of the Kansas Pacific Railway into Denver and built the Denver Pacific to Cheyenne and a connection with the transcontinental Union Pacific-Central Pacific line. The story of gold and silver strikes in western Colorado are legend, but the cost of building standard gauge lines into the canyons and through the Rockies were thought too expensive. Robert Fairlie, who identified himself most prominently with narrow-gauge interests had just presented his paper "The Gauge for the Railways of the Future" before the annual meeting of the British Railway Association. At this time he advocated that a road of 42-inch gauge would be much cheaper to build, equip, and maintain than standard gauge. He also pointed out that a narrow-gauge line, with sharp curves was well adapted to mountainous regions or could be used in areas where traffic was light.

General William J. Palmer called on Robert Fairlie while honeymooning in England. Palmer explained about his proposed railroad to run along the eastern side of the Rockies to El Paso, with Mexico City as the eventual terminus, a distance of 1,600 miles from Denver. For a railroad of such magnitude, Fairlie recommended to Palmer that he consider three-foot as a most practical gauge. To construct and equip a railroad of this size would cost approximately one-third less than a standard gauge line and there would be better utilization of motive power and rolling stock for its comparable size, according to Fairlie. Palmer was sold on three-foot gauge and became its greatest advocate in America.

When Palmer returned to Colorado he organized his Denver & Rio Grande Railway as a three-foot line. The actual construction of the road was started in 1871 and by April of that year a sufficient quantity of iron rails was on hand from Liverpool to lay 30 miles of track. The first spike was driven at Denver on July 28. By the end of September, 43 miles were completed, and the line was opened to Colorado Springs, 75 miles from Denver, on October 27. A complete story about the construction of the D&RG narrow-gauge is presented in a forthcoming section.

Railway engineers from all over the world came to examine this new railroad phenomenon. By 1874 nearly 1,700 miles of new three-foot gauge line had been built in the United States. The total had increased to 2,862 miles by 1878 and the 1880 trackage figures showed that 5,200 miles (or more than five percent of the national total) was of the new gauge. The March 1901 issue of *Railway Age* claimed there were 10,000 miles of common-carrier and industrial narrow-gauge tracks in the nation and 2,000 of them in the Rocky Mountain states of Colorado and New Mexico.

A great deal of literature was published on the advantages of the American narrow-gauge. One of the most popular was *Narrow Gauge Railways in America* by Howard Fleming, a Philadelphia railroad supply dealer. His book was first published in 1875, followed by a second edition in 1876. Much of what Fleming had to say first appeared in the material from Robert Fairlie. In the *First Annual Report - Denver & Rio Grande Railway* that was published in April 1873, Palmer remarked about the narrow-gauge principle and its relation to his D&RG. Another advocate of narrow-gauge was J.T. Davis, President of the Nevada & Oregon Narrow-Gauge Railway, later known as the Nevada-California-Oregon Narrow-Gauge Railroad. He wrote *Narrow-Gauge Railroads: Their Origin, Progress, Success and Benefits* in 1880. Each one of these men presented the seven principles as set down by Fairlie.

America was ripe for something new and cost-saving at the time narrow-gauge was being pushed. When the Denver & Rio Grande was built as the first railroad into the territory, it was implied that other railroads wishing to connect would also choose narrow-gauge and thus form a network of lines. The D&RG was also building into an area of little population, a region of new farms, and a growing cattle industry. Although the mines were booming at the time, the industry was very unstable, but Palmer was headed for El Paso! At the time the narrow-gauge idea was being sold, very few standard gauge railroads in the American West were operating at full capacity. Freight trains were short and in many cases freight cars were at half or three-quarter full most of the time. The contents of one standard gauge car partly full, nicely filled a narrow-gauge car to capacity.

The initial cost of construction and operation certainly interested railroad promoters. Many were under the premise that costs were proportional to gauge. Trunk line railroads were also building narrow-gauge appendages to their systems — Union Pacific, Colorado & Southern, Chicago & North Western, Milwaukee Road, and Atlantic Coast Line. It had been assumed that only narrow-gauge tracks could penetrate the forbidding Rockies and was the answer for light traffic lines. Very little time was given to the probable costs of transfer between gauges as labor was cheap. Palmer was also under the assumption that nearly 80 percent of all traffic on his Denver & Rio Grande Railway would originate and terminate on-line. As his slim rails spread like webs of steel into the canyons and around mountains, this soon proved to be a myth.

When reading the following considerations for selecting narrow-gauge as presented by Fairlie, Fleming and others, these principles made sense and seemed to possess several notable savings and advantages. All were told the narrow-gauge idea was to save hundreds of thousands of dollars in construction and operating costs because it was inherently more compact.

1. *Construction:* The cost of construction is equal to the width of the gauge. In rough mountainous country the narrow-gauge would be greatly less than the proportion to its width. In flat, level ground the proportion would be more.

2. *Cost of Working:* Every inch added to the width of construction, beyond what is absolutely necessary for traffic, adds to the cost of construction, increases the proportion of dead weight carried, and increases the cost of working.

3. *Dead Weight Problem:* The proportion of non-paying to paying weight is increased as the rails are spread further apart. A freight car weighing less than three tons could carry a load of eight tons, or three times its own weight in revenue freight. An engine with 15 x 18-inch cylinders and 36-inch drivers would have a tractive effort on a level grade sufficient to move 1,460 tons, and would have 1,064 tons of freight on a narrow-gauge, while the same engine on standard gauge would haul only 900 tons of freight, as the engine and cars, unloaded, make a total of 566 tons, as against 400 tons on the narrow-gauge. A narrow-gauge train could haul 18 percent more goods everything being equal.

4. *Cost Savings:* There is a decided savings in the original costs of construction equal to 33 percent, owing to the flexibility of the gauge. A narrow-gauge would allow the road to be built very close to the natural contour of the country, which in turn creates a reduction in gradation, bridging and superstructure. Palmer, who was involved in the construction of two standard gauge lines, claimed the cost of construction of standard gauge was $9,520 per mile as against a cost of $3,191 for narrow-gauge. He calculated that the D&RG would only have to do a business of $158,000 per annum in 1873 to be a paying investment.

5. *Capacity:* Engineers in 1875 furnished evidence that established the fact that standard gauge possessed a capacity far greater than the need of the time. In his annual report Palmer stated that the Massachusetts Railroad Commission stated in 1875 that the average number of passengers to each standard gauge passenger train was 71. Taking a train consisting of four coaches, this produced an average of 18 revenue passengers to each car built with a capacity of 56 per car. If each car weighed 35,000 pounds, this would give an unproductive weight capacity of 2,000 pounds transported to haul each passenger. In a narrow-gauge car weighing 15,000 pounds the passenger capacity was 36 passengers. Assuming the car carries only 12 passengers per car, being the same proportions as 18 to 15; the unproductive weight of 1,250 pounds is carried for each passenger, being 750 pounds less dead weight per passenger than standard gauge.

6. *Operating Cost:* The costs of operating narrow-gauge trains was set at under that of standard gauge. In 1873 the D&RG reported the ratio of expenses to gross earnings at 50.2 percent, and for 1874 of 56 percent. In comparing wear and tear the advantage was in favor of narrow-gauge, with its light locomotives and rolling stock. The use of narrow-gauge claimed no advantage over standard in the matter of grade, except that its trains had less dead weight to carry.

7. *Safety:* The narrow-gauge system was considered to be considerably safer than standard gauge due to the lower center of gravity and slower rates of speed on the lighter rails which followed the general upgraded contours of the land.

These claims made for narrow-gauge were appealing. Working from the premise that construction and operating costs were proportional to gauge, many operators found narrow-gauge produced no savings if the traffic volume was not there.

Locomotives built for narrow-gauge railways conformed to the same principles as those for standard gauge, except for the size. The first locomotive built for narrow-gauge use was erected by Smith & Porter Locomotive Works in 1867 for an industrial line of 42-inch gauge. Porter built 50 narrow-gauge engines for industrial use before the Baldwin Locomotive Works built their first narrow-gauge engine in 1868. This was an 0-4-0 tank engine for industrial purposes. The Baldwin Locomotive Works built the first narrow-gauge engines for a main line common carrier in 1871. These were for the Denver & Rio Grande Railway and two classes of power were built; the 2-4-0 type for passenger service and the 2-6-0 Mogul type for handling freight. The passenger engines were equipped with 40-inch drivers, had 9 x 16-inch cylinders and weighed 25,000 pounds loaded. The freight engines had 36-inch drivers with 11 x 16-inch cylinders, and weighted 35,000 pounds loaded. Both types were equipped with a swinging pony truck with a single pair of wheels in front of the cylinders. The 2-4-0 type were found to be too light and small for passenger service, and were prone to leave the track easily owing to their comparatively short wheel base. The 2-4-0 type was abandoned in favor of the 4-4-0 American type locomotive. By 1872, air brakes had been installed on all narrow-gauge engines.

The 4-4-0 and the 2-6-0 remained the prime power for all narrow-gauge lines of America until Balwin offered the 2-8-0 Consolidation type in 1877. This type was first designed in 1866 for the Lehigh Valley, a standard gauge line, but was not offered for narrow-gauge service until 1877. After that time the Consolidation became the workhorse of most narrow-gauge railways. Motive power remained miniature standard gauge engines until 1886 when the Baldwin Locomotive Works offered a 2-4-2 locomotive with outside frames for the Antofogasta Railway of Chile. While we are not primarily concerned with foreign narrow-gauge engines, this was a radical change in narrow-gauge design. Most of the motive power used on the Denver & Rio Grande Western narrow-gauge following World War II all had outside frames. The application of outside frames provided a greater width of firebox between the frames, offered a wider cradle to house a larger boiler, and created greater engine stability due to the outside journal bearings.

Many outside frame narrow-gauge engines were exported by Baldwin, but not a single engine of this design was sold to an American narrow-gauge line until 1901. At this time the Crystal River Railway purchased two 2-8-0's and a third engine in 1903. The Catskill & Tannersville, a New York narrow-gauge, purchased a 2-6-0 and another in 1908.

Very few new narrow-gauge engines were built after 1890 due to the availability of good second-hand power.

These engines had been made surplus when many narrow-gauge railroads converted to standard gauge. The Denver & Rio Grande was loaded with surplus narrow-gauge power and did not order any new engines until 1903, when the road acquired 15 2-8-2's with outside frames from the Baldwin Locomotive Works. These engines were of special interest as very few Mikado's were in service in the country at the time. The D&RG was more or less forced into purchasing the heavier narrow-gauge engines to help move the tonnage ascending Marshall Pass between Gunnison and Salida. Heavier 2-8-2's, also with outside frames, were purchased in 1923 from the American Locomotive Co., and from the Baldwin Locomotive Works in 1925. Additional 2-8-2's were rebuilt from standard gauge engines by the Denver & Rio Grande Western shops in 1928 and 1930.

There was some concern among narrow-gauge railroad men whether the small cars could carry the same class of freight as a standard gauge car. Here again, the narrow-gauge freight equipment was a miniature of a standard gauge car. By capacity a narrow-gauge car carried approximately one third less by volume. As has already been mentioned, very few standard gauge cars ran to full capacity at the time. In transfer of freight the contents of a partly filled standard gauge car nearly, or completely, filled a narrow-gauge car. Narrow-gauge cars also held more, for its size, due to its compact strength and dead weight ratio.

The first eight-wheeled narrow gauge freight cars constructed in America were built by Billmeyer & Small of York, Pennsylvania. The Denver & Rio Grande had requested the builder to submit designs for box cars and flat cars just prior to the start of construction. The designs were approved and the new cars arrived in 1871. In time the firm became a prime builder of all types of narrow-gauge rolling stock.

General Palmer wrote the following in his first annual report of the Denver & Rio Grande Railway. "It will be seen that the one admitted deficiency of narrow-gauge roads — that they are different from existing ones, and prevent interchange of through business — is about to be removed." What Palmer had in mind was the direct interchange of narrow-gauge with standard by means of replacing the trucks of the small cars for standard gauge trucks. During the era of wooden freight cars, the replacement of trucks brought the car sills to the same height. Many narrow-gauge cars were dispatched all over the country during this period, especially refrigerator and stock cars, when standard gauge cars were small and light and trains were short. These cars were held together by a simple coupling device known as the "link-and-pin." Shortly thereafter, an automatic coupling device was invented, but narrow-gauge lines were slow in making the changeover. The Denver & Rio Grande received automatic couplers on passenger rolling stock and then on freight cars between 1903 and 1904. At the time there was no way to couple a "link-and-pin" car to a car equipped with a Janney automatic coupler. From that time on transfer of cars between gauges was limited or until narrow-gauge cars were equipped with the automatic knuckle equipment.

The transfer of narrow-gauge cars to standard gauge was simple enough, but the operation of standard gauge cars on narrow-gauge track was limited due to clearances of cuts, bridges and tunnels.

With the conversion of the Denver & Rio Grande main line to standard gauge, a third rail was applied to much of the trackage in the interim, or until a complete changeover could be made. Standard gauge cars were handled by narrow-gauge locomotives, or vice-versa, by means of a Miller hook or a three-position "link-and-pin" coupler between the two gauges. In more modern times an idler car was used on the dual gauge trackage. This unique vehicle took into account the offset center of the coupler between the two gauges. Narrow-gauge engines handled standard gauge cars by this means for years between Alamosa and Antonito and at the other three-rail terminals such as Salida and Montrose.

The substitution of car trucks between narrow and standard gauge was no easy task. In the beginning cars had to be jacked up and trucks substituted. This feat was made easier by the application of the Ramsey Patented Freight Car Transfer System developed in 1880. This system included dual tracks down in a low pit to accommodate both narrow and standard gauge trucks. On each side of these tracks ran an 18-inch wide track on a raised elevated structure. The car to have its trucks switched ran down on the transfer, was quickly jacked up high enough so as to come to rest on the 18-inch rails which supported the car body during the truck exchange. Ramsey claimed trucks could be switched in four minutes time with his appliance.

Transfer could also be accomplished by overhead crane where the car is lifted in the air, the trucks rolled out and the standard or narrow-gauge trucks substituted. The East Broad Top used this overhead crane method since 1933. The D&RGW also used this method to change the trucks on "Gramps" brand tank cars at Alamosa.

The success of the first steel box car built by the Carnegie Steel Co. in 1894 for standard gauge service did not lead to any substitution of wood for steel on the narrow-gauge lines. Many carriers did acquire steel flat cars, hopper cars, and tank cars for service, and many of them were hand-me-down converted standard gauge cars of small size converted for narrow-gauge use. The exception were the East Broad Top hopper cars acquired in 1913 for coal and silica service. The EBT acquired many steel hopper cars new over the years. To the writer's knowledge there never were any steel box cars built for an American line. Narrow-gauge lines in Mexico and Central America did acquire steel equipment following World War II.

The first narrow-gauge passenger coach in this country was completed in July 1871 by Jackson & Sharp of Wilmington, Delaware, for the Denver & Rio Grande Railway. Named *Denver,* it was built on the conventional pattern like comparable standard gauge coaches, and divided into smoking and non-smoking sections; with two seats on one side and a single on the other. The car had a passenger capacity of 35 revenue passengers. The exterior was painted chocolate brown in color with gold ornamentation and lettering. Jackson & Sharp delivered this car along with coach *El Paso* and two baggage cars shortly after the first rails were laid. Two additional coaches were delivered to complete the order for six cars.

When the Denver & Rio Grande was in the design stage, General Palmer looked to the English engineering fraternity for precedence in rolling stock design. It was Palmer's idea to order several hundred four-wheeled cars, like those on British railways for use on his new narrow-gauge system. After looking at the plans, the Jackson & Sharp firm refused to build such small cars claiming them to be impractical. Palmer was insistent they would work and convinced Billmeyer & Small to accept an order for 10 4-wheeled coaches and baggage cars and a lot of 100 4-wheeled freight cars consisting of 14 and 17-foot flat cars and a group of box cars. The flat cars were used for hauling rail and track construction supplies, and could substitute for coal cars by the installing of portable sides. While these little cars served well in construction work, they were too light for serious freight hauling and they disappeared off the roster by 1880.

The history of narrow-gauge passenger rolling stock was short lived. After the initial flurry of equipping a new line, orders for new replacement coaches evaporated as many of the lines soon converted to standard gauge. Surplus equipment was offered for sale to operating lines at modest prices. The design of narrow-gauge passenger rolling stock was a direct copy from the technology of the standard gauge counterpart. Most of the cars had open platforms and all those cars that survived over the years were either completely rebuilt or upgraded through the years. In fact, the D&RG kept its wooden cars in service for 87 years. A few of the better cars were rebuilt with vestibule ends in 1937 for the modernized service on the *San*

Only by visual comparison can the reader fully comprehend the difference in size between standard and narrow-gauge. (RIGHT) At Owenyo, Southern Pacific No. 18 pulls alongside standard gauge locomotive No. 3203.—GUY L. DUNSCOMB COLLECTION. (BELOW) A D&RGW narrow-gauge box car looks like a toy alongside a 1930 vintage standard gauge wood box car on a siding at Montrose. — ROBERT W. RICHARDSON

Juan and *Shavano* trains.

Sleeping cars operated by the Pullman Company ran on the Denver & Rio Grande and other Colorado lines between 1882 and 1902. When the D&RG pulled up the narrow-gauge third rail between Denver to Alamosa and Denver to Salida, all sleeping car service was then handled by standard gauge Pullmans.

The popularity of the D&RGW's *Silverton* train forced the construction of several steel coaches in 1963-64 and 1978 to accommodate the passengers as the old wooden cars which had been rebuilt so many times were falling apart. Most of these new steel cars simulated the old wood type cars with their open platforms. One had to examine the cars to tell the difference as the sides were scribed to look like wood grooved together.

The application of narrow-gauge to railways in this country was a failure. The narrow-gauge railroads never fulfilled the expectations of their promoters to become the most economic and dominant form of railroad transportation. General William J. Palmer, the advocate of the narrow-gauge principle in this country, was the first to admit the complete failure of the three-foot gauge. By the time the Denver & Rio Grande had merged to form the Denver & Rio Grande Western, the system had evolved into a standard gauge bridge line running between Denver and Ogden via Salt Lake City. The Colorado mining boom was over and the narrow-gauge lines were fighting to pay fixed costs.

While there was a savings in the original construction costs of narrow-gauge lines, there was little savings in the physical plant or operating costs. It cost the same to build a railroad station, water tank, or a roundhouse or shops. Any bridge had to be of equal strength to support a train of given weight. A narrow-gauge train carried the same crew members who received the same wages. The clerical help was the same and labor costs in track repair and maintenance were the same. The capital investment in narrow-gauge was unjustifiable, unless the road to be built and operated was so located that it could never suffer competition or had sufficient traffic to pay fixed costs.

The narrow-gauge idea was pushed to its extreme in this country by the construction of two-foot gauge trackage in the state of Maine. No matter whether the gauge was two-foot, three-foot or 42-inch gauge, there is little in American railroad history that holds a greater appeal to the railroad enthusiast or historian than narrow-gauge. The White Pass & Yukon is the last American common-carrier line that still operates complete freight and passenger service daily. And so — twilight has descended upon the narrow-gauge railroads of America, but their appeal as an authentic museum piece will live on forever.

Table of Contents

The sounds of crossheads and reciprocating siderods announce the arrival of an empty coal train at the Great Aughwick River crossing near Pogue, bound for Robertsdale and the mines. — JOHN KRAUSE

1

East Broad Top

The earliest tracks were laid to carry coal to Newcastle. The first locomotive to run in America was intended to haul coal from mine to canal. The railroad, in its beginning, was an adjunct to the business of mining, and so it was with the East Broad Top Railroad.

Residents of Aughwick Valley proposed the construction of a rail line along the banks of Aughwick Creek, a meandering stream which drains the water of the fertile valley south of Mount Union into the Juniata. The railroad would transport the products of the huge stone iron furnaces of Rockhill Furnace, lumber from Broad Top Mountain, and farm products from the Valley. The outcome was the organization of the Drake's Ferry & Broad Top Railroad Company in 1849. Drake's Ferry was an early name for Mount Union, but in any case no further action was taken as the nation was plunged into a five year Civil War.

Following the war, the East Broad Top Railway & Coal Company was incorporated May 24, 1871, under the laws of Pennsylvania, to construct a railway from Mount Union, on the Pennsylvania Railroad, to Robertsdale, a distance of 30 miles. Construction got underway early in 1873 and the first 11 miles between Mount Union and Rockhill Furnace were open to traffic on August 30, 1873. The road began to haul the products of the local iron furnaces and farm products.

At Rockhill Furnace, the road built an extensive shop complex and enginehouse to house its six locomotives acquired from the Baldwin Locomotive Works. No. 3, a 2-8-0 had been built for the Denver & Rio Grande as their No. 13, the *Mosca.* Before delivery to the D&RG it was found to be too heavy for the road's rails, so Baldwin repainted the engine and delivered it to the EBT. By 1875 the road had two 2-6-0's and three 2-8-0's. The line was also equipped with two coaches, two baggage cars and 149 revenue freight cars.

Once the facilities at Rockhill Furnace were established the construction crews moved south toward Pogue, Three Springs and Saltillo. To this point on the line the maximum grade had been 140 feet to the mile, and was continuous for three miles, the average grade being 80 feet. South of Saltillo the road got into mountain country which involved blasting a four percent grade up the side of the rugged Broad Top Mountain. Two tunnels were bored through ridges to keep the roadbed from becoming even more trecherous.

With the mountain section completed, the track layers pushed the steel rails toward Robertsdale. In the meantime the Rockhill Iron & Coal Company was formed to mine the Broad Top coal after taking over the Rockhill Iron furnaces. The first train load of cars started down the line to Mount Union from Robertsdale on November 4, 1874.

Now that the main stem was complete, management took stock and began to make improvements to its physical plant. Many of the smaller trestles were replaced by fills, and additional locomotives were added to the roster. Spur tracks fanned out to mining operations and two more main line stations were established beyond Robertsdale — Woodvale and Alvan.

While many narrow-gauge lines were considering the conversion to standard gauge in order to compete, or were subject to a "boom" or "bust" economy, the EBT seemed to sail along at a steady course. She was able to hold her own until the mid-1950's.

Like all turn-of-the-century carriers, the EBT had asperations of stretching out. The road planned to extend a line east from Rockhill Furnace to Burnt Cabins via Shade Gap. The EBT made an agreement with the Cumberland Valley Railroad to meet its rails at Cowen's Gap. While grading continued at a furious pace it stopped nearly overnight when it was learned that Vanderbilt planned to invade the territory. The EBT lacked the influence for that kind of competition and it all would end in a senseless rate war to which the EBT would lose. The road had no choice but to abandon its expansion plans. While the EBT suffered heavily financially, it was able to recoup some of the loss by handling agricultural products and lumber over a portion of the completed section.

Robert S. Seibert, a local boy who made his fortune in western railroads, returned in 1903 to purchase control of the East Broad Top. He had begun his railroad career 29 years earlier as an EBT ticket agent. He would completely rebuild the road from the ballast up including heavy steel for the iron rail, wood trestles replaced by steel spans, and the substitution of steel cars for the old wooden equipment. The Rockhill Furnace shops also continued to keep pace with every modern innovation as the road began to construct its own rolling stock. One of the first concrete arch bridges in the nation was built over Aughwick Creek near Aughwick. At the time concrete was still in its infancy as a construction medium.

The railroad's first big power came in 1908 when Seibert ordered No. 11, a 2-6-2 Prairie type, from the Baldwin Locomotive Works. The new engine worked so well on the up-graded track that additional power was ordered in 1911, the first of six Mikado type 2-8-2's, also from Baldwin. The new power helped to eliminate frequent double-heading of coal trains. Previously 10 trains a day — five each way — had been necessary to handle 1,000 tons of coal down Broad Top Mountain.

The EBT did yoeman service during World War II and upon the conclusion of this emergency, all locomotives were retired save the six Mikados and the two standard gauge 0-6-0 switchers which worked the transfer at Mount Union.

With the passing of the steam locomotive on standard gauge lines, railroad historians and buffs took a renewed interest in the steam operated East Broad Top Railroad. This new traffic was not enough to preserve the line's passenger train which was abandoned in 1953.

Following World War II more and more industries began to switch from coal for fuel to furnance oil and natural gas. While a bit more expensive, it was less dirty and no clinkers had to be shoveled. Before long operations on the EBT were sharply curtailed. Also one of the silica brick plants at Mount Union closed which also hurt traffic. Before long the service was cut down to one train per day - five days a week. On November 30, 1955 the road applied to abandon the 32.63 miles of main line between Mount Union and Alvan. Besides the Rockhill Coal Company was planning to terminate its coal shipments on March 31st the following year. Permission to abandon was not long in coming. The last train order was issued on Friday, April 6, 1956.

The East Broad Top Railroad was sold to the Kovalchick Salvage Company and everyone expected the railroad to be only a memory in a few months. Nothing happened except that rust gathered on the rails and grass grew between the tracks. For four long years the railroad sat idle, the grass grew, died, then came up again the next spring.

The bi-centennial of Orbisonia (next to Rockhill Furnace) was to be held in 1960. The celebration committee approached Nick Kovalchick to see if it would be possible to reopen a portion of the line and offer train rides. The management was willing to cooperate.

After months of fixing up the track, locomotives and rolling stock, the East Broad Top Railroad was once again in business as No. 12 handled the first train on August 13, 1960 over 3.5 miles of track out of Rockhill Furnace. Railroad buffs and regional citizens came from out of the woodwork. Trains were packed every day and when the bi-centennial was over they continued to come on weekends. Before long the trackage was extended and additional trips run, especially in the summer. Today, the EBT trains cover five miles of the original line, yet the steel is still in over the 32 miles from Mount Union to Alvan. Each year interest grows in the old narrow-gauge. Before long maybe the whole railroad will once again see polished rails caused by the passage of excursion trains!

At the standard gauge transfer at Mount Union, No. 17 is cut from its coal train and suddenly the tender trucks drop to the ground. On an adjoining track, standard gauge switcher No. 3 shifts a narrow-gauge caboose. — JOHN KRAUSE (LEFT) The crew then returns to switch coal hoppers. — PHIL HASTINGS (BELOW) Back on the rails, No. 17 leaves Mount Union with a load of empties for the mines. — JOHN KRAUSE

A long drag of 50 empty coal hoppers, and a combine at the rear, steam near Rockhill Furnace. The white steam of the whistle signal is carried over the top of the locomotive and the coal hoppers. — JOHN KRAUSE

Coming south from Mount Union, No. 17 eases across the pioneer cement bridge over Aughwick Creek at Aughwick. (OPPOSITE PAGE) A touch of winter remains on the ground in this scene, as No. 16 steams southbound along Aughwick Creek near Shirleyburg located between Mount Union and Rockhill Furnace. — BOTH JOHN KRAUSE

After a snowstorm, No. 17 moves a train of empties a few miles north of Rockhill Furnace. — JOHN KRAUSE (ABOVE) Engine No. 14 and train top the grade at Rockhill Furnace. — PHIL HASTINGS

South of Shirleyburg, two trains have a meet. No. 17 on the siding at the left, signals No. 18 which steams up and prepares to pass. The two crewmen at the center throw the switch when the southbound passes. (RIGHT) The driveway bridge leading to a farm crossing over the tracks between Rockhill Furnace and Shirleyburg, long a favorite for photographs, was the locale for this shot. — BOTH JOHN KRAUSE

Just in from Mount Union, a short train of only 10 cars pulls into Rockhill Furnace. The yard tracks are aglow with the wildflowers of late spring. — JOHN KRAUSE

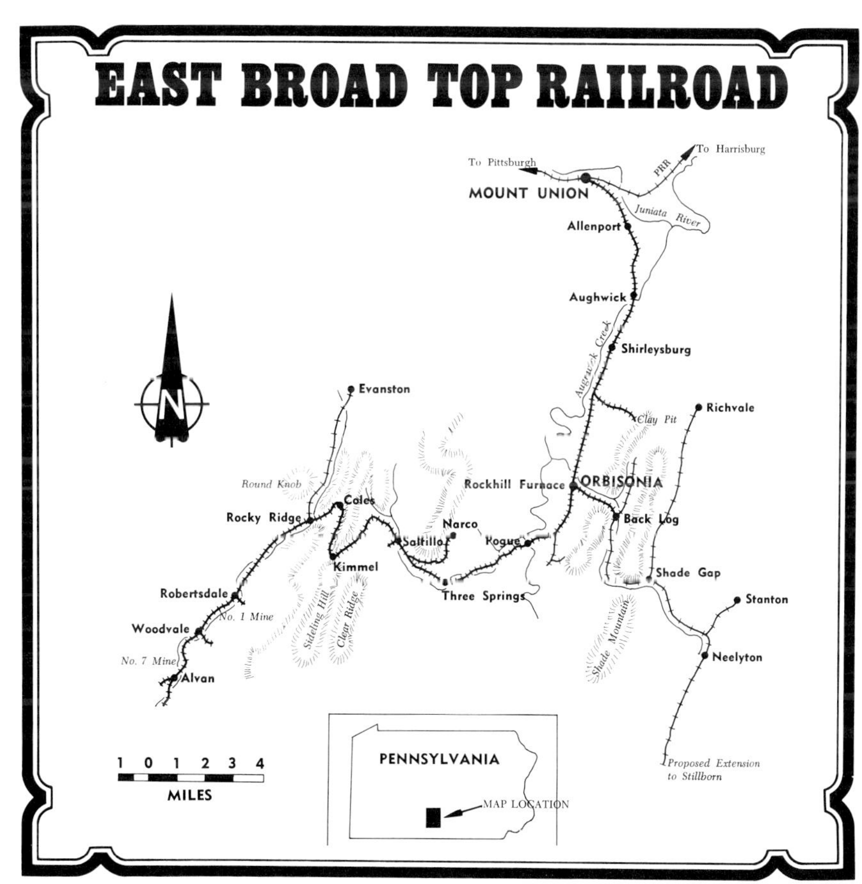

Engine No. 15 spots coal at the coaling tower at Rockhill Furnace yard. EBT's only tank and scale test car are in the foreground. — PHIL HASTINGS (RIGHT) Freight train steaming past the station at Rockhill Furnace. — JOHN KRAUSE

The Rockhill Furnace yard and shop were home to the road's six Mikado's. In this scene, No. 16 moves slowly through the yard en route to Robertsdale. Note the three way stub switch at the left. — JOHN KRAUSE (RIGHT) The conductor picks up orders at Rockhill Furnace, as the train heads for Mount Union. — PHIL HASTINGS

No. 18 is in the shops at Rockhill Furnace for its annual inspection. At the right, No. 16 is in process of receiving new flues. — JOHN KRAUSE

The machine shop of the East Broad Top was most complete. All major and minor repairs to locomotives and rolling stock was accomplished here. (RIGHT) No. 15 is in the roundhouse at Rockhill Furnace. Huge steel doors kept out the winter's cold. — BOTH JOHN KRAUSE

Extra No. 15 heads north with silica rock for fire brick from the NARCO branch, and was photographed at speed near Pogue. NARCO is the abbreviation for the North American Refractories Company. — PHIL HASTINGS

Locomotive No. 15 pulls a string of antique varnish over the Aughwick Creek bridge near Pogue, three miles south of Rockhill Furnace — ROBERT W. RICHARSON (OPPOSITE PAGE) No. 16 clatters across the steel viaduct, longest span on the EBT, near Pogue. — JOHN KRAUSE

E. B. T.

Crisp morning cold holds the steam from the stack and the steam dome as No. 18 rolls through Three Springs headed for Saltillo and Robertsdale. — JOHN KRAUSE

The engine crew takes on sand the hard way as they scoop it up from a boxcar on a siding at Saltillo during the winter of 1955. (BELOW) Two trains pass at Saltillo? One would gather a passenger train is on the main line and a freight coming off the NARCO branch, but this is not the case. It is all one train, the crew using the combine car for a caboose. The EBT had only two cabooses and chose to use the more comfortable combine after the abandonment of mixed train service. — BOTH JOHN KRAUSE

Heading toward Mount Union from Saltillo with No. 10 and a load of firebrick silica. Note the near perfect reflection in this field full of rain water and melted snow. — JOHN KRAUSE

Locomotive No. 17 pulls up to the water tank at Saltillo. This was one of several enclosed tanks protected with a shed around it to keep the contents from freezing. Other tanks like this were located at Mount Union and Robertsdale. — JOHN KRAUSE

The East Broad Top had two tunnels on its line. One was located at Kimmel and the other at Rock Ridge. In the scene on the opposite page No. 17 blasts through the north end of Kimmel tunnel. Large steel doors were placed on the northern end of each bore for use during the winter. Each door was controlled from a switch along the track near the south end of each bore. The engineer would trip the switch and when the door was raised a green light would show at the south portal. — JOHN KRAUSE

On a cold winter day, No. 16 with 41 loads up from Robertsdale rolls to the portal of Kimmel tunnel and stops. She holds the main at the southern end of the bore. Before long the thunder of No. 18 can be heard as she enters the northern end of the tunnel and then blasts through as she moves onto the siding in order to pass the train of loads. — BOTH JOHN KRAUSE

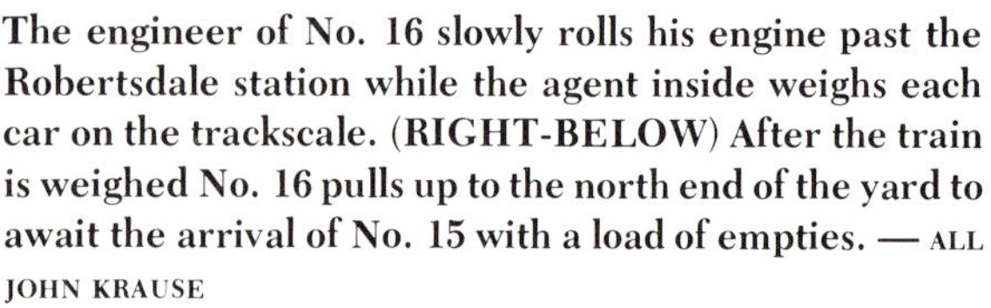

The engineer of No. 16 slowly rolls his engine past the Robertsdale station while the agent inside weighs each car on the trackscale. (RIGHT-BELOW) After the train is weighed No. 16 pulls up to the north end of the yard to await the arrival of No. 15 with a load of empties. — ALL JOHN KRAUSE

The termination of mixed train passenger service in 1953 also ended the use of the road's classic gas-electric rail motor car built in EBT's own Rockhill Furnace shops from Brill and Westinghouse parts in 1927. The motor car was used to make weekend passenger and mail runs at times when coal trains did not run due to the mines being slow, or during strikes when there were no coal trains at all. (LEFT) The front end of M-1 resembled a Brill motor car. (BELOW) The motor car at Robertsdale, waiting for the return run to Rockhill Furnace. — BOTH JOHN KRAUSE

Loading mail aboard M-1 at Robertsdale. — JOHN KRAUSE

The EBT had only two cabooses and here they are passing each other at Cook's Siding, near Robertsdale, in 1952. — PHIL HASTINGS

Engineer Frank Rinker, a man who spent most of his life on the narrow-gauge, stands alongside an old friend. (RIGHT) No. 16 and the combination car turn on the wye at Robertsdale. — BOTH JOHN KRAUSE

Engine No. 16 and combination car at Robertsdale after cutting out the empty hoppers from the mixed consist. In this scene, the agent in unloading mail and express. — PHIL HASTINGS

Mount Union yard with No. 18 and the old combination car at the enclosed watertank. Standard gauge 0-6-0 No. 6, built by the Baldwin Locomotive Works in 1907, is moving down to the engine shed. — JOHN KRAUSE

EBT No. 12 in the yard at Rockhill Furnace, just south of the shops, during the first year of tourist operations. Note the enlcosed sand tower alongside the water plug. — JOHN KRAUSE

At Robertsdale, No. 16 holds down the main line while No. 17 has just turned on the wye. The station is located just behind where the photographer took his illustration and to the left. (RIGHT) The drivers of No. 17 spin as she bites into the rails while pushing a train of empties up the NARCO branch. — BOTH JOHN KRAUSE

With a clear track ahead all the way to Rockhill Furnace, the engineer cracks open the throttle on No. 15 as it leaves Mount Union with a five car excursion train. (BELOW) Private car No. 20 was still in first class condition as it brought up the rear of the excursion train. Rumor has it that President Grover Cleveland used this classy vehicle on his fishing trips. — BOTH ROBERT W RICHARDSON

The last train on the East Broad Top ran on April 6, 1956. It went from Rockhill Furnace to Saltillo, up the NARCO branch for some loads of ganister rock, returned to Rockhill Furnace and then on to Mount Union. In this scene, agent/operator Scott is handing up orders for the last run — a roundtrip to Mount Union. — JOHN KRAUSE

E B T Today

The East Broad Top came back to life on August 13, 1960, with the first train operation in four years. While the excursion trains only cover about five miles of the original main line, the steel rails still extend 32 miles from Mount Union to Alvan. The passage of time has done little to the EBT except to magnify its historic interest. (LEFT) The repainted No. 14 on the turntable at Rockhill Furnace ready for the opening day. (BELOW) The tourist train behind No. 12 pulls into the yard at Rockhill Furnace in 1969. — BOTH JOHN KRAUSE

Baldwin built No. 11 is dramatic and thundering as she rolls along at the bottom of State Line Hill grade headed for Cranberry, North Carolina. Due to declining revenues this was the final day of operation — October 16, 1950. — JOHN KRAUSE

2

East Tennessee & Western North Carolina

The East Tennessee & Western North Carolina Railroad (Tweetsie), was the first railroad to cross the Blue Ridge. Her narrow-gauge rails opened up mountain country which had known only isolation and remoteness since the days of the Indians. In fact, before the railroad, the only way to get to Boone was to be born there.

While searching for "ginsing" root near Cranberry, North Carolina, the Perkins brothers ran into a rich vein of ore. Finding that the vein ran for some 21 miles along the border between Tennessee and North Carolina, there was no way to get it out unless they built a railroad. The East Tennessee & Western North Carolina Railroad Company was organized on May 24, 1866 as a broad gauge (5-foot) railroad to accomplish the transport of the iron ore.

Construction began in the summer of 1898 and the grade was nearly completed between Johnson City and Hampton by the following summer. A bit of track was laid west of Elizabethton and some of the bridge work was completed — but money was running out. The road underwent several changes in ownership, and by the time this road with no rolling stock or locomotives was hardly five miles in length, it was in receivership.

The railroad fell into the hands of Ario Pardee, a Philadelphia businessman, who was a large shipper of anthracite coal. Since he had just purchased the Cranberry Iron Works and formed the Cranberry Iron & Coal Company, he had a stake in the whole region. This acquisition was to be a natural one. After all the legal technicalities had been cleared, construction of the railroad began in earnest in 1879. Pardee quickly saw the advantages of a narrow-gauge railroad to Cranberry, even though part of the line had been constructed to permit the passage of broad gauge cars. With narrow-gauge there would not only be a savings in construction, but in the purchase of equipment. Ahead lay the formidable granite-bound Doe River Gorge of the Blue Ridge Mountains. The cliffs were so steep in places that men had to be lowered by block and tackle to carve out a right-of-way. The line in the region required five tunnels to push the line safely between Elizabethton and Blevens, four were in the gorge itself.

From Hampton to Cranberry, a distance of 20 miles, the railroad climbed 1,500 feet in elevation. As cut after cut were hacked out by hand, and the rubble carried off by pack mule, the cost of the project jumped to over a million. By the time the summer of 1881 rolled around, 15 years after the original charter had been granted, the ET&WNC was in operation between Johnson City, Tennessee, to Cranbery, North Carolina, a distance of 34 miles.

The first locomotive arrived in 1880 and was a Baldwin 2-6-0 (Mogul). Another 2-6-0 followed in

1881, and then came four Consolidations (2-8-0) over the next 22 years. A lone Brooks 0-8-0 appeared in 1906 and followed by a fleet of Ten-Wheelers delivered between 1907 and 1919.

Now that the railroad was completed to Cranberry, this opened up the vast timberlands of the Blue Ridge Mountains. While some logging had taken place it had been limited to mine timbers, acid wood and tan bark. Several railroads had been proposed to connect with the ET&WNC, but it took the three Camp brothers of Chicago to get things rolling. They incorporated the Linville River Railroad on July 13, 1896 to construct a railroad from Cranberry to the mill at Saginaw, North Carolina, approximately 12 miles. After some grading everything stopped. In 1898 the Camps sold their interest to Isaac T. Mann and William N. Ritter who formed the W. M. Ritter Lumber Company with the railroad projected to Pineola.

The major timber holding of Ritter had been logged off shortly after the turn-of-the-century. The Linville River Railroad was of little importance to the lumber firm. The ET&WNC purchased the line on August 1, 1893 which extended its tracks from Cranberry to Pineola, another 12 miles. An extension was built to Shulls Mills in 1916, and a short time later, the road went all the way to Boone — giving the ET&WNC a 66 mile line. It now required four hours running time from end to end.

Now appearing like a mainline narrow-gauge railroad the management equipped its line with vestibuled coaches and parlor cars. While dining cars and Pullman service was not provided, patrons could order meals at each end of the line.

The Blue Ridge Mountains, like New England, was covered bridge country. The bridge just east of Hampton was the site of many classic photographs of smoking locomotives emerging from the 118-foot structure built in 1882. This unusual Howe through truss bridge across the Little Doe River served the line to the end.

By the early 1930's the revenue of the ET&WNC began to drop with all the timber being logged off. In order to save money the company formed a bus service to preserve the passenger service and started a freight trucking line to save what less-than-carload business they had. Somehow the road managed to ride through the Depression. The Tweetsie began to lay a third rail between Johnson City and Elizabethton, a distance of 9.5 miles, in 1904. This was done to accommodate standard gauge cars from the growing business firms up to that point. Standard gauge power was secured to handle this segment of the line.

Due to declining revenues, maintenance on the entire right-of-way was cut to the bone and weeds grew between the ties. After a flood in 1940 nearly washed out the entire Linville section, the line beyond Cranberry was abandoned on March 22, 1941. This left the dual gauge from Johnson City to Elizabethton and the narrow-gauge to Cranberry — the original line. The old narrow-gauge continued to run until September 1950, when approval was given to abandon the narrow-gauge section. The last freight ran on October 16, 1950.

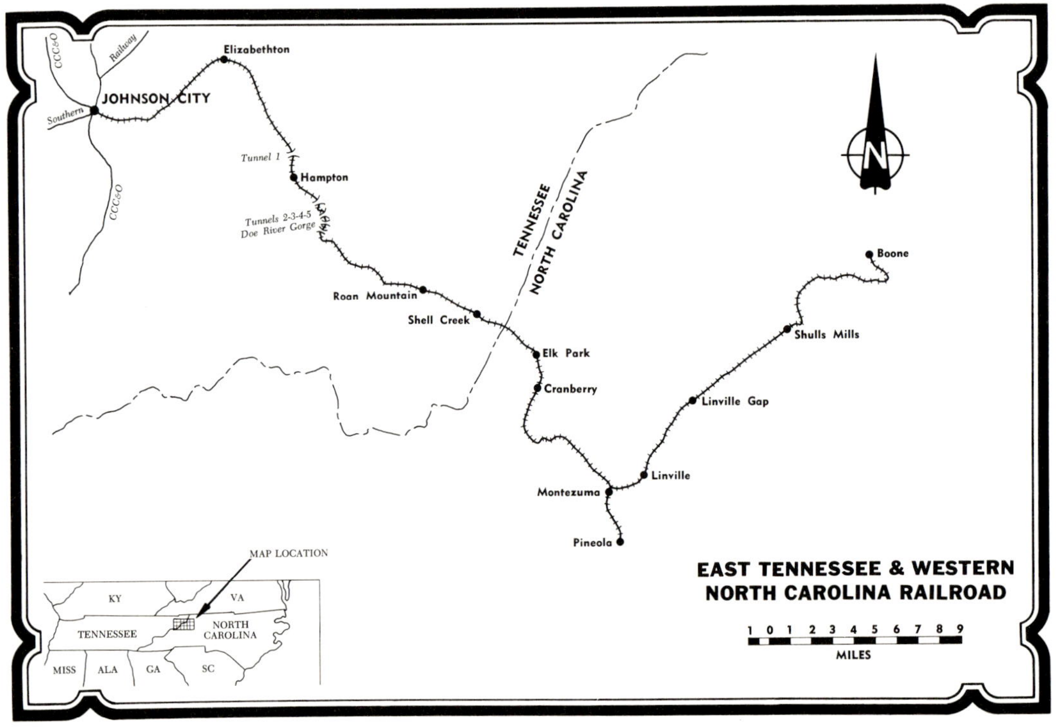

Old No. 11 was showing her age as she steamed away near the enginehouse at Elizabethton. The stains below the smokebox door often hinted of flue leakage. (BELOW) A load of acid wood, used in the tanning of leather, was on the manifest as No. 11 leaves Elizabethton for Johnson City during 1950. — BOTH JOHN KRAUSE

Under a rolling cloud of smoke, No. 11 moves across Valley Forge bridge just outside of Elizabethton. — JOHN KRAUSE

Engineer Fred Helton runs No. 11 eastbound through the classic Howe Truss covered bridge spanning the Little Doe River located a half-mile out of Hampton, Tennessee. It's a wonder the cinders from all those engines didn't set the structure afire once in a while! — JOHN KRAUSE (RIGHT) The twisting trackage of Doe River Gorge contained four tunnels and here No. 11 works upgrade out of tunnel No. 4 and then clatters across a steel bridge. — ROBERT B. ADAMS

A mile and a half from Shell Creek, Tennessee, ET&WNC No. 11 works State Line Hill east on a fill of iron refuse rocks on the last revenue run. — JOHN KRAUSE

Engineer Brownie Allison brings ring stacked No. 11 eastward through Elk Park, North Carolina, in high style. (BELOW) Nearly topping State Line Hill, the track levels for about 500 yards and then climbs once again up a 4.5 percent grade into Elk Park itself. — BOTH JOHN KRAUSE

After climbing the 4.5 percent grade, No. 11 passes through a deep cut as it rolls into Elk Park. — JOHN KRAUSE

Shenandoah Central

Following the abandonment of the narrow-gauge East Tennessee & Western North Carolina, engine No. 12 and two coaches were shipped to a Virginia farm where they operated on the privately owned Shenandoah Central Railroad at Penn Laird. The train operated on a one mile loop during the summer months. On October 15, 1954, the fringe of Hurricane Hazel dumped 7 inches of rain on Penn Laird in 12 hours. The rush of water destroyed most of the right-of-way and the railroad ceased operation. (RIGHT) No. 12 crosses a small stream at Cub Run. — H. REID (BELOW) The train at Massaniten Summit. — AUGUST THIEME

Tweetsie

Lumberman Grover Robbins purchased the rolling stock and locomotive of the Shenandoah Central and moved the railroad to Blowing Rock, North Carolina, in 1955. Here he built this Tweetsie Railroad, a 1.5 mile route complete with heavy cut and fill work, a steep grade, and a wooden trestle 225 feet long and 50 feet high. The following year a three mile loop was completed and a railroad station erected. (ABOVE) Maintenance crews fill the sand dome of No. 12 at Blowing Rock. (LEFT) The smell of coal smoke and hot lubricating oil fill the air along the rhododendron-flanked right-of-way of Tweetsie. — BOTH H. REID

Ely Thomas Lumber Co. No. 5 brings a Sunday afternoon train along Mann's Run to Jetsville, West Virginia. The company provided transportation to the woods camp for workers with a Shay complete with a number plate which defied placement, and a hose around the sand dome for emergency purposes. — AUGUST A. THIEME

3

East Coast Industrials

The industrial narrow-gauge railway was cradled in the mountains of North Wales, and owes its existence to the slate industry which began to expand in the 1830's. In order to move larger quantities the quarry owners began to use narrow-gauge tram-roads with horses for power. The Festiniog Railway, built and opened in 1836, was the first industrial steam operated railroad line specifically engineered for an industrial purpose. One might classify the Festiniog as the *Godfather* of the American industrial narrow-gauge.

Who built the first narrow-gauge industrial railroad in the United States remains a mystery today. We do know that Smith & Porter Locomotive Works built its first narrow-gauge industrial locomotive in 1867 for the New Castle Railroad & Mining Company of Pennsylvania. The engine was an 0-4-0T engine of 42-inch gauge. Porter had built 50 narrow-gauge industrial engines by 1868 when Baldwin built its first narrow-gauge industrial engine for the Averill Coal & Oil Company of West Virginia. This engine was also an 0-4-0T of 42-inch gauge. Bear in mind the first locomotive built for a main line narrow-gauge railroad did not come until 1871 when the Baldwin Locomotive Works built the engines for the Denver & Rio Grande.

An industrial railroad is rather hard to classify as it can be a common-carrier railroad, yet serves only one industry. In any case, an industrial narrow-gauge is one that generally is not a common-carrier and transports a single product. It may or may not physically connect with any other railroad. The road was used primarily in industrial plants, in the mining industry, for logging and switching around lumber mills, and all types of service to agriculture such as cane railroads, etc. Industry chose narrow-gauge because it saved both in the cost of construction and the purchase of locomotives and rolling stock. Industrial railroads continued to be projected until the coming of the motorized truck which was more versatile and not relegated to stay on specific tracks. The truck, however, could not compete with rails when the item to be transported is in any given volume. Even today the application of the industrial railroad is unlimited if the volume justifies the expense of the initial physical plant.

A perfect example of narrow-gauge railroads in industry was in logging. Several hundred narrow-gauge loggers were built in the West, and more than half of these were located in California. The last commerical line was the famous West Side Lumber Company line which is described in this book.

One of the last busy narrow-gauge mining railroads in the United States is U.S. Gypsum's line at Plaster City, California. This road still operates five days per week and is also described later.

The industrial lines presented here are primarily in the eastern sector of the United States and are mainly concerned with coal and log transportation. These are a few that survived the period following World War II.

Lehigh Navigation

The Lehigh Navigation Coal Co., a name significant in the Pennsylvania anthracite industry operated a 42-inch mine-to-coal separator line with hefty tank engines. The separator at Lansford removed the slate, shale, rock and dirt from the raw coal. While slower to ignite than bituminous, Lehigh coal once lit, provides a hot, and relatively smokeless flame. (LEFT) A strong arm was needed to put an empty hopper back on the track. (BELOW) No. 84, at the bottom of the incline, runs past No. 83 pushing unculled coal to the separator. — ALL JOHN KRAUSE

Up, up, up, and, chugga-chug, toddles No. 84 with a pusher at the rear. (LEFT) A chain-drive Bulldog Mack truck shares the water spout with a steamer. — JOHN KRAUSE

Abridged-chimneyed No. 37 rends the air with the rattling of four-wheeled empties as the little hoppers, with link and hook couplers, make their way back to the mine. The American Car & Foundry Co. cars were capable of carrying three short tons each. Lehigh found nearby Vulcan Iron Works at Wilkes-Barre convenient for power. These 0-6-0's function with 27½ x 24-inch cylinders, 190 pounds steam pressure, 42-inch drivers and 27,000 pounds tractive effort. (BELOW) The Lansford separator and yard with cars traveling up and down the incline to and from the crusher/separator. — BOTH JOHN KRAUSE

Gray Lumber

The Gray Lumber Company, located at Waverly, Virginia, was an anachronism of the time. Dual gauge surface bent tracks, push carts, and four wheeled cars pulled by mules operated at the mill of this Central Virginia timber operator. When the East Tennessee & Western North Carolina sold their No. 8 in 1920, she finished out her days hauling logs for Gray Lumber. In the scene below, No. 8 handles a two-car train of timber and rolls through the Waverly yard. When progress did catch up in the fifties, a lot of mules went on the unemployment roles. — ALL H. REID

Dismal Swamp Railroad

The Dismal Swamp Railroad's No. 1 had all but finished hauling out timber from the gum and juniper glades when H. Reid photographed her in November 1947. The underslung 42-incher stands on a storage track at Camden Mills, Virginia, awaiting the scrapper.

Richmond Cedar Works

The Richmond Cedar Works near Suffolk, Virginia, was an isolated operation lasting but a few years after World War II. This Porter product of 42-inch gauge tended Ryland Camp cuttings. The No. 8 incorporated the standard eastern Virginia accessories of pilot beam sand box and tender water syphon, and operated on rails whose grade characteristics could not be calculated by miles but, by each length of track. — H REID

Ely - Thomas Lumber Co.

Lumbering is still going on deep in the woods of West Virginia, but all the Shays are gone except for those in tourist service. In the above scene, just beyond the clapboard logging community of Jetsville, No. 5 and a quaint home-constructed utility car trailing, cross a span locally identified as the "big bridge." Ahead, but out of view, was an enginehouse for one locomotive. — AUGUST A. THIEME

Shay No. 5 brings in a load of fresh cuttings to the log dump at Jetsville. From here the logs were transhipped in standard cars to the Ely-Thomas mill at Fenwick in Nicholas County. — BOTH D. WALLACE JOHNSON.

Babcock Coal & Coke

The Babcock Coal & Coke Co. shunted coal in wooden hoppers from the tipple at Clifftop, West Virginia, to the Chesapeake & Ohio reload at Sewell. In the view above, Shay No. 8 steams along nearly three miles out of Clifftop on a private excursion. (RIGHT) Wheezing steam at Clifftop, No. 8 waits for a load of coal for the C&O transfer. (BELOW) Switching cars at Clifftop. — ALL AUGUST A. THIEME

Argent Lumber

The Argent Lumber Company had a rare and fascinating operation at Hardeeville, in the southernmost part of South Carolina. Seven woodburners operated as the Argent Tramway and switched the narrow and standard gauge cars at the mill and hauled logs by trains over a 25-mile line into the Georgia swamps east of Hardeeville. The line had four 2-6-0's, one 2-6-2, and two 2-8-0's. The operation became inactive in 1956 and abandoned in 1959. (FAR RIGHT) No. 7 a Porter 2-8-0 with engine No. 1, another Porter of 2-6-0 wheel arrangement at Hardeeville. — MALLORY HOPE FERRELL (CENTER) No. 7 moving out with a train of logs. (BELOW) Passing in the swamps near Hardeeville. — JIM SHAUGHNESSY

Under a rolling cloud of smoke and cinders, the *Silverton* train climbs the grade near Rockwood en route to Durango. — JOHN KRAUSE

4

Denver & Rio Grande Western

General William J. Palmer was the creator of the Denver & Rio Grande, Rio Grande Western, Mexican National railroads, the founder of the city of Colorado Springs, and the pioneer of the narrow-gauge system in the United States.

In order to fully comprehend how the narrow-gauge idea came about it is necessary to understand the man that brought it all about. Palmer was born September 17, 1836 in the state of Delaware of Quaker parents of modest means. During his early childhood his parents returned to Philadelphia. There he entered school and excelled in all engineering type subjects. By the age of 17 he launched out into the world, joining the engineering corp. of the Hempstead Railroad then under construction in Pennsylvania. He switched to the Pennsylvania Central (later Pennsylvania Railroad) where he gained invaluable railroad experience from J. Edgar Thompson, a great railroad builder of the time, and fellow Quaker.

F. H. Jackson, Palmer's uncle, an associate of the growing Westmoreland Coal Company of Pennsylvania, informed his nephew his firm was seeking a young man to study England's railroad and coal operations and present a report of his findings. Young Palmer, only 19 years of age, was selected to make the journey in 1855. He returned a year later and was appointed secretary of the firm based on his outstanding presentation.

The Pennsylvania Railroad, in the meantime, had been formed with his friend Thompson as its third president. Under Thompson's management the road grew and prospered. At this time wood was still used as locomotive fuel, although coal-burning engines were being considered. Thompson had read Palmer's report on English coal-fired steam locomotives and hired the young engineer to develop a coal-burning firebox and to test an engine using various grades of coal. The experiments were undertaken at Altoona with Andrew Carnegie as his associate. Before testing had been completed, the nation was thrown into a Civil War. Carnegie stayed with the railroad and later became the road's superintendent of the Western Division prior to engaging in his own steel making activities.

T.A. Scott, fellow Quaker and family friend, was appointed Assistant Secretary of War in charge of transportation for the Union. Knowing Palmer's knowledge of railroads he employed the young man to join his supervisory staff. Palmer reluctantly chose to join the 15th Pennsylvania Cavalry and acquired the rank of Captain. He quickly advanced to Colonel in 1863 and was promoted to Brigadier General just before Lee's surrender. Thus William J. Palmer acquired his famous title of "General".

After the war Palmer's mind returned to railroading. His friends, Thompson and Scott, were interested in the progress of the transcontinental railroad project and attempted to interest Palmer in this "Great Work of the Age". Knowing Palmer's strong ties with Pennsylvania, Thompson explained that the future for a young man was in the West.

Palmer chose to take on the construction of the Kansas Pacific, a line pushing west across the plains along the 35th parallel, rather than associating himself with the Union Pacific. He was appointed treasurer of the firm in 1865 and in the spring of 1867 he associated himself with the KP survey crew who planned to make a trip to the Rocky Mountains and the far west seeking a route to the Pacific. It was during this adventure that the seed was planted for the projected Denver & Rio Grande Railway.

While a member of the survey team, Palmer met a Dr. William A. Bell, an Englishman, who acted as photographer. He not only took pictures, made sketches and wrote a log of the adventure, but at the end of the survey published his notes in the famous book *New Tracks in North America* which is used as a primary source for the look of the old West.

The survey crew explored various passes across the Rockies including Raton Pass, and the countryside around the Sangre de Cristo Range to the origin of the Rio Grande River. They explored the Royal Gorge and found it was possible to put a railroad through the canyon. Moving west they studied the routes along the 32nd and 35th parallels concerning possible extensions of the Kansas Pacific to San Francisco. When the survey was completed, Palmer would issue his own report and analysis of the venture entitled *The Report of the Survey Across the Continent.*

All this time the Kansas Pacific continued building toward Denver. While not heavily involved in the construction of the road at the time, Palmer was becoming famous in the east as an engineer, soldier, railroad builder, and now pioneer of the West. On his return Palmer was placed in charge of construction of the road between Sheridan, Colorado and Denver, plus the Denver Pacific Railway from Denver to Cheyenne and a connection with the main line of the Union Pacific. With the completion of these projects, Palmer, not yet 35, turned to his own plans and projects.

The wealthy citizens of Denver were already talking about a railroad on the east side of the Rockies between Denver and Trinidad. The proposed railroad as chartered was called the North-South Railroad. When the charter was withdrawn, Palmer was quick to grab it. His desire to build a railroad along the eastside of the Rockies began while on the survey team and was privately revealed months before the Kansas Pacific line reached Denver. Colorado businessmen were enthusiastic, but European capital was needed to get the project beyond the talking stage.

Palmer returned to Pennsylvania where he married Mary Lincoln "Queen" Mellen and the two journeyed to England for a honeymoon. During his visit to the British Isles he visited Fowler and Stacey, two famous railway engineers who had built narrow-gauge railways in India; he also visited with chief engineer Charles E. Spooner of the Festiniog Railway of Wales. Spooner had just written extensively about the building of the two-foot gauge line in his book *Narrow-Gauge Railways.* Palmer also visited Robert Fairlie, an internationally known British railway expert and locomotive designer. He suggested to Palmer that he considered three-foot gauge as the proper width for this proposed railroad in mountainous country. He explained such a gauge would be 37 percent cheaper in initial cost and was perfectly balanced for adhesion. Palmer was convinced. While there would be much discussion on the question in years to come, he never faltered from his conviction to three-foot gauge.

While in Wales, Palmer ordered enough 30 pound rail to complete a line of railway 90 miles in length. Upon the invitation of his good friend Dr. Bell, he visited the wealthy of England and Holland for subscriptions to his proposed railway. The good doctor was also out circulating among his father's rich clients, attempting to interest them in a promising Western railroad investment. William P. Mellen, his wealthy father-in-law, was raising funds in America among the eastern capitalists.

Returning from Europe, Palmer had enough subscriptions to formally organize his railroad. The company was incorporated on October 27, 1870, in Colorado, as the Denver & Rio Grande Railway to construct a railroad from Denver to El Paso, on the border with Mexico, and to Mexico City, a projected distance of 1,720 miles, of which 850 would be in the United States. The line was to be built by the Union Contract Company without any governmental subsidy.

The company officers agreed that the railroad should be built as a three-foot gauge line as opposed to the four-foot eight and one-half inch gauge known as standard. Several reasons were given for making this decision. First, the complete acceptance of the narrow-gauge idea by General Palmer. Second, it was believed at the time that the line would run through mostly mining and agricultural country and the bulk of the freight traffic would originate and terminate on-line. Since there were no other railroads south of Denver, the gauge of the D&RG would dictate the track width for all subsequent carriers in the region. The use of narrow-gauge would mean cheaper construction costs in terrain requiring considerable rock work, expensive excavation, and frequent tunneling. This factor was believed to be of interest to British investors who were already familiar with the gauge. The initial purchase price of locomotives and rolling stock was also in direct relation to the width of the track. Narrow-gauge could offer better utilization of space in freight cars as most standard gauge cars never ran to 100 percent capacity.

The line was to run south from Denver to Pueblo via Colorado Springs, and on into New Mexico territory by way of Canyon City, Poncha Pass, the San Luis Valley, the Rio Grande basin, and extending to El Paso. Here the line would be met by the rails of the Mexican National building north from Mexico City. This plan was first suggested as a branch line for the Kansas Pacific as proposed in the survey made by Palmer in 1867. Another line would run south from Pueblo to Trinidad, tap the coal fields at El Moro, cross the Sangre de Cristo Range at Raton Pass and connect with the main line at a selected point. Other lines were planned to include one into the South Park region and another up the Arkansas River to Leadville, both if possible to be extended across the mountains into western Colorado, and on to Salt Lake City.

The first spike on the D&RG was driven July 28, 1871 in front of the new Denver Union Depot. Company attorney Samuel Browne predicted that within 20 years all railroads in the country would be narrow-gauge. The following day the first three-foot gauge track in America was put in place so that three narrow-gauge locomotives and flat cars could be unloaded to form the first construction train. The first passenger train ran three miles to end of track on August 14, consisting of a locomotive, two baggage cars, two smoking and non-smoking coaches named *Denver* and *El Paso*. By the end of September, 43 miles of track were completed and the line was opened to Colorado Springs, 76 miles from Denver on October 27.

The first train to enter Pueblo, the old Santa Fe Trail trading center 118 miles from Denver, was on June 10, 1872. A branch to Lubran, site of large coal deposits near Canyon City was commenced before the main line built into Pueblo, and reached there in October.

It began to appear that the D&RG's eyes were bigger than its pocket book. The treasury was always low and the directors in attempting to save time and money figured they would cut at least 100 miles off the line to El Paso by running the line south of Pueblo to Cucharas and cross the Spanish Range at La Veta Pass rather than going through the Royal Gorge. By 1874 some 40 miles of roadbed were graded between Pueblo and Cucharas, building toward Trinidad. The extension to the coal fields at El Moro (near Trinidad) would double the line's gross business, and there were over 100,000 head of cattle grazing in the nearby mountains waiting for shipment east. Trinidad was also a junction point on a profitable east-west wagon road that should offer traffic to Denver. Then to the west lay the rich silver bearing San Juan Mountains also in Colorado.

By late 1877 the D&RG had convinced itself that it had sufficient grasp upon southern Colorado and New Mexico so as to make other rail competition unlikely. The San Luis Valley and the San Juan Country were theirs by virtue of the line over La Veta Pass to Fort Garland and the planned extension to Alamosa. The merchants of Santa Fe watched the slim tracks push toward El Moro and Raton Pass. This would take the D&RG over the old Santa Fe Trail to the great trading center of the American West.

The Atchison, Topeka & Santa Fe Railway had aspirations of using Raton Pass. On February 26, 1878 the president of the road authorized William Strong to go ahead with construction toward Santa Fe and the West. Strong directed his chief engineer, then in Pueblo, to lay claim to the pass as quickly as possible. A. A. Robinson boarded a Rio Grande train and headed for El Moro where, after the train arrived, he rented a horse and rode to "Uncle Dick Wootton's house in the pass. He made an offer and obtained control of his toll road. On the same train was D&RG's chief engineer John McMurtrie with the same idea in mind. He failed to recognize Robinson on the train and felt no urgency to get to Raton Pass. He spent the night in El Moro and lost nearly a full day getting to Wootton.

The Santa Fe gained control of Raton Pass and also obtained an injunction from the court prohibiting the sharing of the pass with the "Baby Road". Blocked at this point, Palmer realized he could not finance a legal battle with his larger foe. He also pulled back for fear the Santa Fe might strike out for Leadville via Canyon City.

Another controversy between the D&RG and the Santa Fe did occur with the attempt of the Santa Fe to build northeast from Pueblo and Canyon City through the Cañon of the Arkansas River, known as the Royal Gorge. The Santa Fe had reached Pueblo in 1876 with its standard gauge, while the D&RG was already in Canyon City at the Lubran Mines. It appeared the aim of both roads was to reach the silver mining region in which Leadville was situated. The Royal Gorge was so narrow that it was impossible for two railroads to build through it without serious problems. After many disputes and much litigation, the courts decided in favor of the D&RG, and the Santa Fe withdrew.

The D&RG fell on hard times financially and the road was leased to its arch enemy, the Santa Fe, on December 1, 1878, for a period of 30 years. The Santa Fe immediately halted further expansion and began to manipulate rates over the D&RG in an attempt to win its traffic war with the Kansas Pacific, which connected with the D&RG at Denver. Such tactics would destroy the D&RG and its source of income. Palmer went to court in protest and the road was delivered to a receiver.

Jay Gould had secretly been purchasing D&RG stock with the thought of using the line to punish the Santa Fe for its rate actions against his Kansas Pacific. Gould was powerful enough to dictate a peace between the parties, and he lost no time doing so by threatening the Santa Fe with parallel construction along its lines if they did not back down. All court actions were terminated and the receiver discharged. On March 27, 1880 the D&RG was free to pursue its destinies with Gould's backing. The road embarked on its narrow-gauge expansions into western Colorado. This is fully described in the following sections of this volume. It is not the intention of the author to present a complete history of the Denver & Rio Grande, but for the sake of the story we need to explain a few happenings.

The disadvantages attending the use of narrow-gauge were now becoming apparent, especially where the D&RG connected with standard gauge railroads at Denver and Pueblo. Interchange of traffic at these points was expensive and inconvenient. Accordingly, in 1881, work was started on laying a third rail from Denver to Pueblo, so that both narrow and standard gauge rolling stock could be handled. The dual line was opened in January 1882. Since there was no time to build a wider roadbed the third rail was simply spiked to a longer tie inserted in the existing narrow-gauge track.

The completion of the narrow-gauge line to Salt Lake City was effected in April 1883 and the following month was extended to Ogden, Utah, 771 miles from Denver. While reaching its primary goal, the D&RG began to face many discouraging periods in its career. It was located in a sparsely settled country and was carrying a heavy bonded indebtedness. The mines were not providing the road with the revenue it had anticipated and the road was further handicapped by reason of its being narrow-gauge. The railroad, located in mountainous country with steep grades and sharp curves, was difficult and expensive to operate, and was subject to heavy snow, washouts, etc. Palmer was losing his control and resigned as president in 1883.

The following year the road was in receivership once again, there were mergers and foreclosures until the establishment of the Denver & Rio Grande Western Railroad as we know it today.

Since the Denver & Rio Grande was the first three-foot gauge railway, it is interesting to take a look at the motive power development over the years. The first locomotives were built by the Baldwin Locomotive Works, and were of two types — the 2-4-0 for passenger service, and the 2-6-0 Mogul for freight. The details of their construction were quite similar, and interchangeable parts were used wherever practicable due to limited shop facilities. The boiler shells and tubes were of iron, and the fireboxes of steel; and bituminous coal was used as fuel. At this time no one was aware of the excellent grade of anthracite coal at Crested Butte. The smokeboxes were short, and the stacks were of the diamond pattern. The tenders were of the four-wheeled design; those for the passenger locomotives carried 500 gallons of water, and for the freight locomotives 750 gallons. The locomotives were not large, so they obviously had to stop often for fuel and water.

At the time the road was opened, the passenger schedule allowed five hours for the run between Denver and Colorado Springs, a distance of 76 rail miles, this being the equivalent of a speed of 15 m.p.h. Bear in mind this run was made on newly constructed track not yet settled and the rail weight was only 30 pounds per yard.

During the years 1871 to 1873 four passenger locomotives were built, and eight Moguls for freight. The last five Moguls had fireboxes six inches longer than the first three; and two of these engines had two steam domes each. The boilers had a straight top which was extensively used by Baldwin at the time.

With the completion of this power in 1873, the rolling equipment of the road consisted of: 12 locomotives, 7 passenger cars, 4 baggage, mail and express cars, 4 open excursion cars, 258 freight cars, 22 dump cars, 21 hand and push cars, plus snow plows.

Early in 1876 a large class of Mogul was received from Baldwin. As compared with the first Moguls, the cylinder diameter was increased and the boiler enlarged. The tenders on these engines were of the eight-wheel type, with a capacity of 1,200 gallons of water. Eight engines of this design were built during the years 1875 to 1878.

As the system grew, additional power was required. The 2-4-0 type passenger engines proved too light for the work to be done; and three 4-4-0 American type engines were built in early 1876 by Baldwin.

In 1876 work began on the lines from Cucharas, over La Veta to Fort Garland. The line crossed the Rockies at 9,339 feet, and had grades of four percent and curves of 30 degrees. Baldwin built an experimental 2-8-0 Consolidation type called *Alamosa* in 1877 for use on the line and represented the largest and heaviest narrow-gauge engine built at the time. The engine was highly successful on the heavy grades, and traversed the sharp curves with little flange wear. It established the Consolidation type as standard power on the narrow-gauge for years to come. At the close of the 1882, a total of 128 Consolidations were built by Baldwin for the Denver & Rio Grande. Three sizes of cylinders were represented, viz: 15 x 18, 15 x 20, and 16 x 20 inches. In the majority of cases they were of the straight-top type.

During 1881 and 1882 the D&RG experimented with 28 Consolidation type locomotives, with 15 x 20-inch cylinders, built by the Grant Locomotive Works. This was the largest single order from a locomotive builder other than the Baldwin Locomotive Works until the turn-of-the century.

Eight engines of the Ten-wheel type were secured in 1882 from Baldwin, followed by 12 additional engines between 1883 and 1884. Four of the engines were placed in passenger service between Denver and Pueblo enabling the D&RG to make the run in five hours. The locomotives were reported to curve and ride easily.

In 1883 Baldwin built three narrow-gauge 4-4-0 American type engines to burn Colorado anthracite coal from Crested Butte. The engines were placed on the Salida-Gunnison line, and later switched to operations out of Grand Junction. As hard coal burners they were a failure, as they could not run for more than a few miles without failing to steam. These were the only engines on the road built to use such fuel. Since this experiment, bituminous was used on all narrow gauge engines.

The decision was reached in 1881 that the narrow-gauge could not economically compete with the major standard gauge lines. The inability to make direct interchanges was the basic reason for the conversion of the line to standard gauge between Denver and Salt Lake, plus the arm to Trinidad. This decision was made in such haste that narrow-gauge engines on order were widened to standard gauge width. This change left the narrow-gauge lines with an over supply of power. No new engines were required until 1903.

Fifteen engines of the 2-8-2 Mikado type were built by Baldwin to assist increasing traffic over Marshall Pass. They had Vauclain compound cylinders, and developed a tractive force, working compound of 25,700 pounds. The boiler had a wide firebox, placed back of the drivers and above the rear truck; and the frames were outside the wheels to insure sufficient stability on three-foot tracks. These engines with greatly increased power were subsequently partially rebuilt and fitted with single expansion cylinders and slide valves. Several of these engines were fitted with superheaters and piston valves.

Over a period of 20 years a lot of the original small power with at least 50 years service now required extensive repair to remain in service. Heavier rail on the Marshall Pass line and over Cumbres permitted heavier motive power. In 1923 the American Locomotive Company built ten freight locomotives of the 2-8-2 Mikado type developing 27,540 pounds tractive force. These engines with superheated steam were equipped with Walschaerts valve gear. The frames were also outside the wheels and all drivers were flanged. These engines were later relegated to passenger service most of the time.

Two years after these engines were placed in service, ten additional engines of the same type, but considerably greater in capacity, were built by Baldwin. These engines with 143,850 pounds on drivers, developed a tractive force of 36,200 pounds. Like their predecessors, they used superheated steam, had outside frames and Walschaert valve gear.

The last engines to appear on the Denver & Rio Grande Western narrow-gauge were ten 2-8-2's converted from 1902 Baldwin built standard gauge engines in the company's Burnham Shops during 1928 and 1930. These engines were also the most powerful narrow-gauge engines on the Denver & Rio Grande Western system.

Alamosa to Chama

An eastbound mixed freight works its way along Wolf Creek Valley, crosses a graded dirt highway called Colorado 17, then continues the ascent of Cumbres Pass as it nears Coxo. — JOHN KRAUSE

This photographic story of the D&RG narrow-gauge begins at Alamosa, the largest and most important town in the San Luis Valley. It is a large potato shipping center and the official headquarters of the narrow-gauge lines. The locomotive and car shops for the entire system are located here. The town was founded in 1878 by former Governor A. C. Hunt, president of the Denver & Rio Grande Construction Co. The location in the center of the valley was an ideal junction for the various lines. (ABOVE) Narrow-gauge power handling the local switching duties at Romero on the 28 miles of dual gauge line to Antonito. Note the idler car behind the second engine. — DONALD DUKE (RIGHT) Excursion train passing through LaJara, 14 miles south of Alamosa. — JOHN KRAUSE

Livestock is in profusion in western Colorado. Here a cattle drive not only stops traffic on the narrow-gauge, but highway traffic on U.S. 285 running between Alamosa and Santa Fe. In this 1954 scene, and excursion train returns to Alamosa, and is on the outskirts of town. — JOHN KRAUSE

A Durango bound excursion train at Antonito, junction of the line to Santa Fe and the Cumbres Pass route to Durango. This location is the chief shipping point for a large agricultural region and end of the dual gauge trackage. — JOHN KRAUSE

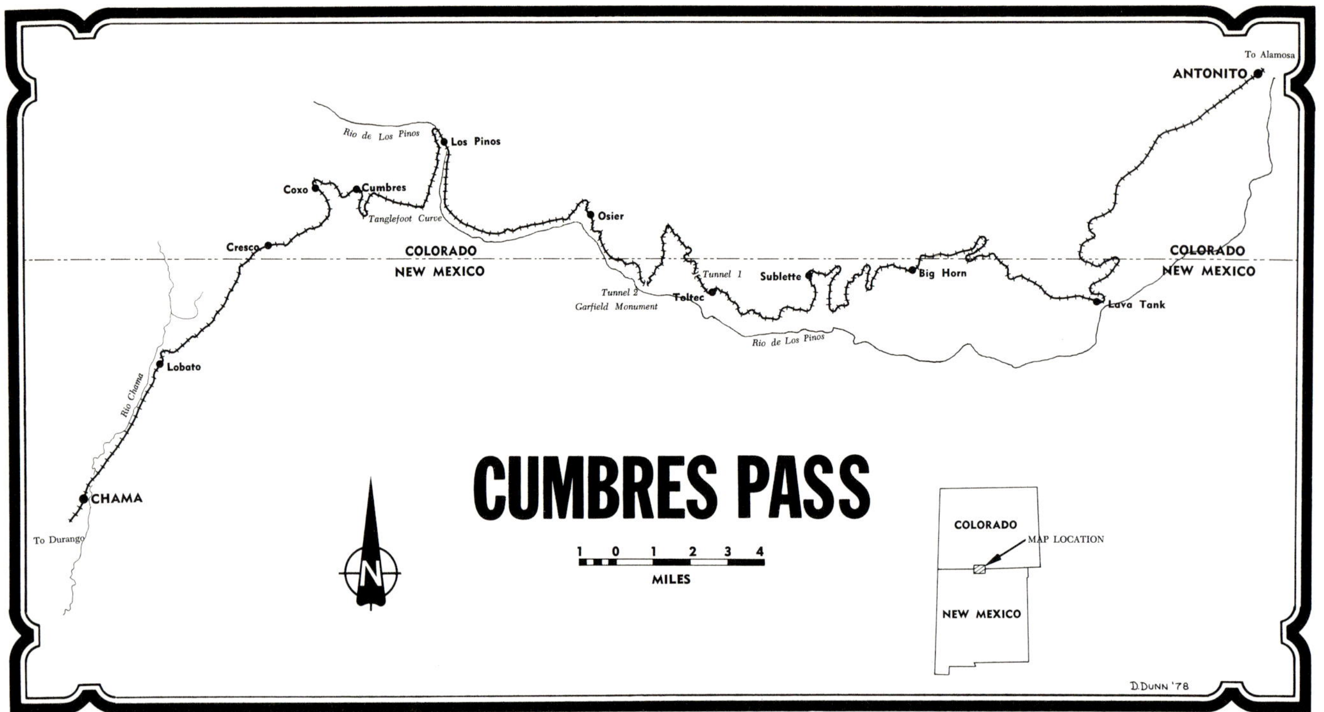

The story of rails over Cumbres Pass began on October 24, 1879, when construction engineer Robert F. Weitbrec got together with D&RG chief engineer J. A. McMurtrie in Pueblo to plan the San Juan Extension. On February 20, 1880, the construction crews began to lay track from the railhead at Alamosa to Antonito. Here the railroad simultaneously built two lines: one southwest to Santa Fe, the other westward bound for Silverton. The line over Cumbres lay in extremely rough country as is evidenced by the above map. While most trackage followed streams and canyons, this extension cut across from one canyon to another. (RIGHT) A helper drifts through Sublette as it returns to Alamosa after helping a freight from Chama to Cumbres. The helpers always ran ahead of the regular train as they could make the run in half the time. — JOHN KRAUSE

West of Antonito the rails began a long climb of 1.4 percent grade along sagebrush covered slopes to attain the tops of lava-covered mesas. The rails meandered in continuous curves while winding in and out of side canyons north of the Los Piños River. In this scene a stock extra rolls downgrade to Antonito as it nears Toltec. — JOHN KRAUSE

An eastbound freight is about to enter the west portal of the Toltec Gorge tunnel. The stone pillar is the Garfield Monument erected during September 1881 by members of the National Association of General Passenger and Ticket Agents who held a memorial alongside the new tracks in Toltec Gorge when they learned President Garfield had been shot by an assassin. — JOHN KRAUSE

As the new rails climbed toward Cumbres back in 1880, the valley below the tracks grew deeper and deeper and the terrain more spectacular. After passing through the second of only two tunnels on the entire D&RG narrow-gauge, the line burst out over a breathtaking precipice of Toltec Gorge. At this point the rails were more than 800 feet above the tumbling waters of the Los Piños River. (ABOVE) An Alamosa bound helper drifts into the Toltec Gorge tunnel. The substantial rock wall and fill replaced a precarious wood trestle at the turn-of-the-century. (LEFT) Two views of the beginnings of Toltec Gorge near Osier, west of the monument. Here helper No. 492 drifts along toward the tunnel en route to Alamosa. — ALL JOHN KRAUSE

In order to gain elevation for the final ascent to Cumbres, the main line follows the Los Piños River Canyon north two miles from Los Piños siding to Los Piños sectionhouse and tank. At this point the tracks make a long sweeping snakelike loop as they cross from one side of the canyon to the other. (RIGHT) Locomotive No. 491 is assisted by a helper No. 486 cut in the middle of the train as it works around the big loop. Note the flat cars of oil pipe bound for Farmington just beyond the water tank. (BELOW) An eastbound freight which left Cumbres 30 minutes earlier, drifts around Los Piños loop bound for Alamosa. — BOTH JOHN KRAUSE

The westbound freight shown on the previous page at Los Piños tank continues to work hard as it nears Cumbres station. Below the summit the rails make another giant loop, this time in the form of a horseshoe. While the tracks appear to join each other by a switch, the rails are separated by some 20 feet in height. In the scenes on this page, the freight approaches the horseshoe loop. — ALL JOHN KRAUSE

Locomotive No. 486 and a 76-car freight train had been waiting at Cumbres station for over an hour for No. 491 and its Chama bound train to pass. Now that the line to Alamosa was free of traffic, No. 486 and train left Cumbres and was photographed rounding the horseshoe loop. Note the drop in elevation of the loop tracks as is in evidence beside the caboose. (RIGHT) No. 496 which has helped No. 486 and train up the hill from Chama to Cumbres, has turned on the wye, and is about to return to Chama. — BOTH JOHN KRAUSE

High, beautiful, desolate, and windy are words one might say about the summit of Cumbres Pass. In winter the location was pure hell. At the summit of this 10,200 foot high pass, the brakes are carefully checked before No. 491 makes the descent down the 4 percent grade to Chama. The wye at the left is enclosed in a snowshed for obvious reasons. — JOHN KRAUSE

As the train moves west from Cumbres station, the panorama of Wolf Creek Valley below opens up. At this point Chama is 14 miles in the distance. Here the tracks round a giant lava outcropping where the wind blows constantly and is properly named Windy Point. (LEFT) An eastbound freight rounds Windy Point. — DONALD DUKE (BELOW) A freight passing below Windy Point heads for Cumbres station. (OPPOSITE PAGE) An eastbound freight works its way around Windy Point. — BOTH JOHN KRAUSE

Lobato bridge is one of two major steel viaducts on the Cumbres Pass line, and just four miles east of Chama. Due to the extreme weight of the narrow-gauge locomotives, two engines coupled together are not permitted to cross the bridge at the same time. One engine is cut off, run ahead, and re-coupled on the other side of the bridge. (LEFT) The helper engine crossing the bridge.
— BOTH JOHN KRAUSE

No. 495 is on the point of a "Cumbres Turn" as it steams along just three miles from Chama. (RIGHT) A stock extra was photographed heading toward the Cumbres mountains (in the distance). — BOTH JOHN KRAUSE (BELOW) An eastbound freight crosses the Chama River with No. 473 on the head end and steams for Cumbres. The fake diamond stack and the bright orange and black paint are for the pleasure of the tourists when the locomotive is in her usual roll as power on the *Silverton* train. — DONALD DUKE

The Wolf Creek Valley, between Chama and Cumbres summit, presents a most picturesque glen like setting for the photographer. Here the action of Cumbres bound trains and the atmosphere make a rare combination indeed. (ABOVE) Engines Nos. 491 and 499 fill the valley with stack talk as they slowly move a stock extra toward the summit. This scene is just each of Lobato bridge. When the freights were too heavy too handle with three engines, the train was broken up into two sections call "Cumbres Turns." The crews would make a run to Cumbres with the first section, then drift back for the second half of the train. At the far right, No. 486 leads a three engine freight east of Lobato. (RIGHT) No. 473 at the rear helps push the tonnage to the top of the grade. — ALL JOHN KRAUSE

499
499
499
Rio Grande

In the view above, No. 497 works the head end of a long Cumbres bound freight near Cresco. (RIGHT) The same freight west of Lobato bridge headed for Windy Point. (OPPOSITE PAGE) No. 499 with a string of Gramps tank cars appears to be coming right out of the ground as it climbs the 4 percent grade of the west approach to Cumbres. In reality, the train has just crossed Lobato bridge and is slowly making its way to Cresco.
— ALL JOHN KRAUSE

The railhead reached the Chama River on December 31, 1880, and the town named for the river crossing. The town was to become a trading center, substantial lumber town, railroad division point, and helper station for the ascent of Cumbres Pass from the west. Here the D&RG constructed a five stall brick roundhouse, a frame station and coaling facility. By February 1, 1880, the line from Alamosa to Chama was in full operation with freight and passenger service. From this point freight wagons struggled with cargo bound for the San Juan mines, while passengers rode in J. L. Sanderson's stages to Animas City (Durango). Chama continued to be a division point and helper station where live engines were steaming across from the station. In winter the rotary snowplow was on call 24-hours per day in case Cumbres drifted in. Chama became a shipping point for oil when the Chromo Valley oil field opened up in 1937. In the scene above, a freight prepares to leave for Cumbres. No. 495 with caboose will act as helper. (TOP RIGHT) Switching in the Chama yard. (LOWER RIGHT) Helper engines steaming away alongside the enginehouse. — ALL JOHN KRAUSE

Chama

Cumbres in the Winter

Cumbres was in an ideal location to catch drifting snow and every once in a while storms of epic proportions would drop 10 feet of new snow overnight, requiring the service of the rotary. In the days of the daily passenger train, its passage would keep the line clear of drifts. Snow begins to fall in the high country by mid-October and would be on the ground as late as July. There were always deep drifts between Lobato and Los Piños. In the top view, a string of tanks just out of Chama is about to cross Lobato bridge en route to Cumbres. — DONALD DUKE

Wolf Creek Valley is still coated with snow as this extra is photographed east of Lobato. (RIGHT) The same train rounding Windy Point from Coxo.
— BOTH JOHN KRAUSE

The beauty of the Colorado-New Mexico border is in evidence in these scenes. Between Lava and Chama, the rails cross the Colorado-New Mexico border 7 times. (TOP LEFT) No. 494 is so hot she is poppin off while still working hard through Cresco. (LEFT) The same train just below Windy Point. — BOTH JOHN KRAUSE

The pusher rolls back to Chama through Coxo for the second half of the train. Note the road engine on the hill just below Windy Point. — BOTH JOHN KRAUSE

The east end of the Cumbres yard. An eastbound freight is about to continue its run on to Alamosa. (BELOW) A freight approaching Coxo as seen from Windy Point. — BOTH JOHN KRAUSE

Spring was no lamb at Cumbres station. During the winter of 1948 the hill received more snow than the locomotive mounted plows or flangers could handle. The Jordan spreader came to the rescue. This winged device is seen clearing the tracks at Cumbres station while photographer Robert W. Richardson nearly froze his --- while snapping these spectacular scenes.

Engine No. 499 holds back on an empty Farmington pipe train as it makes the Cumbres horseshoe in 1954. Old photographs carrying a historical record at the bottom state this was a "Whiplash" curve. (LEFT) With tracks full at Cumbres, this pusher takes two cars to Los Piños siding for pick-up in April 1954. After making a set-out she will return to Chama. — BOTH JOHN KRAUSE

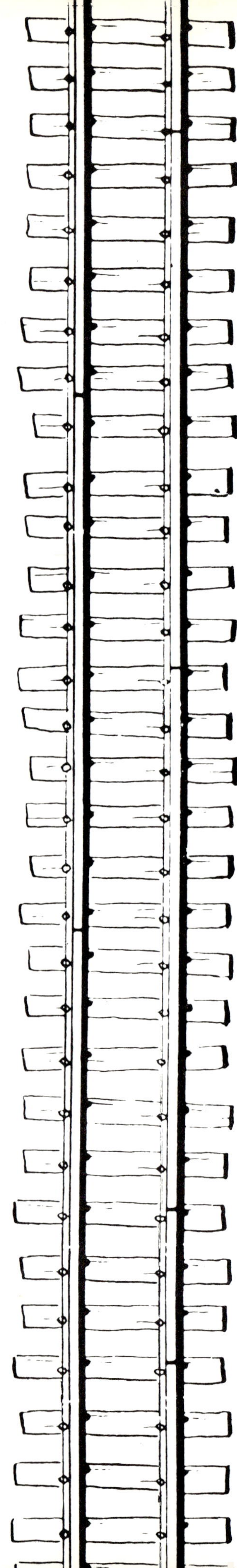

Silhouette of the double-header leaving Chama for Durango.— JOHN KRAUSE

Chama to Durango

The terrain between Chama and Durango was in deep contrast to the lush mountain country over Cumbres. While still in the high country, the green has changed to unusual rock formations and smaller trees. At Monero, 19 miles west of Chama, considerable coal mining takes place. In the scene above, engines Nos. 487 and 494 roll an eastbound through Monero Canyon headed for Chama. (LEFT) The same train deep in the canyon. — BOTH JOHN KRAUSE

The heavy rock outcropping and the scarcity of trees are typical of the region around Monero. In the scene above, an eastbound freight winds through a canyon. (LEFT) In narrow-gauge country, the highway traveler had to keep a sharp lookout for trains. A freight could dart across the road at any time without crossing signal or gates. All one expected to see was the train and hear the whistle. —BOTH JOHN KRAUSE

Arboles, shown on the opposite page, was deep in Indian country. The Utes derived their principal income from sheep, goats and horses, and a little agricultural products. This tank town offered little more than a cold drink, stock pens, and thirst for the locomotive from an old tender turned into a water tank. (RIGHT) A few miles east of Durango, a freight begins the climb out of the Animas River Valley. (BELOW) This Chama bound freight rolls alongside an alfalfa farm at Falfa. — BOTH JOHN KRAUSE

Rio Grande
476

Durango, narrow-gauge capitol of the world! The slim rails finally reached here on July 27, 1881. It was not the end of the line, it was merely a stop on the extension to Silverton. The town of Durango was built in 1880 by the railroad. Its name apparently was suggested by Alexander Hunt, who at that time was traveling in the region of Durango, Mexico, on business for General William J. Palmer, president of the D&RG. This rough and tumble community became a center for the San Juan Basin and major shipping point for cattle, mining and agriculture. (ABOVE) Activity at Durango station with No. 345 about to wye the *San Juan*. — JOHN KRAUSE (TOP LEFT) The parlor car *Chama* at the depot. (LOWER LEFT) The early day *Silverton* at the station. — BOTH DONALD DUKE (OPPOSITE PAGE) Panorama of the Durango roundhouse as photographed from the top of the coal tower. — PHIL RONFOR

485
Rio Grande

The San Juan

Regular passenger service to Durango was inaugurated out of Pueblo shortly after the rails reached there during the summer of 1881. Not until September 25, 1887, did through trains begin running between Denver and Durango as a train called the *Durango Mail.* The service was complete with day coaches, sleepers, dinette and parlor car facilities. Over the years it carried such names as the *Colorado & New Mexico Express* and lastly the *San Juan.*

The *San Juan* known during the last 14 years of passenger operation on the Alamosa-Durango line began in the summer of 1937. The passenger rolling stock was rejuvenated, the old open platforms were enclosed with vestibule ends, electric lights and steam heat replaced the old brass oil lamps and stoves. The coaches were fitted out with modern upholstered reclining seats; the parlor cars were equipped with four-seat dining section and a galley.

The parlor cars *Alamosa, Chama,* and *Durango* kept the open section on the rear end and were dignified with a large electrically lighted drumhead sign inscribed *San Juan*. The normal consist was five cars including a Railway Post Office (RPO), baggage car, two coaches, and a parlor car.

As early as 1915 the automobile began making inroads on passenger traffic, however, the *San Juan* remained the only public service in many areas, especially in winter. Following World War II Lucius Beebe wrote articles in "Holiday" magazine describing this unique train, its leisurely pace and the spectacular scenery. A whole new breed of passenger took to the narrow-gauge cars. The parlor car steward acted as attendant, chef, newspaper delivery man to patrons along the line, plus serving candy and ice cream cones to Indian kids along the Colorado-New Mexico border. The RPO provided daily mail service to this outback region.

On January 31, 1951, the *San Juan* made its final run between Alamosa and Durango. New Mexico having refused permission to abandon the train within the state, required the D&RG to operate a one car stub train from Chama to Dulce on the *San Juan* schedule until May 22, 1951.

In the scene above, the *San Juan* is challenged by the grade lifting the rails out of the San Juan Basin near Durango. — ROBERT W. RICHARDSON (OPPOSITE PAGE) The *San Juan* in 1950 running toward Durango about five miles east of town. At this time the train had been cut by one coach. — JOHN KRAUSE

In its last year, 7 o'clock was train time at the Alamosa station. As the narrow-gauge locomotive coupled up, and tested the air, the *San Juan* was ready to leave for Durango. — CORNELIUS W. HAUCK

At 8:05 the *San Juan* pulled into Antonito, one time junction with the line to Santa Fe, New Mexico. — R. B. JACKSON

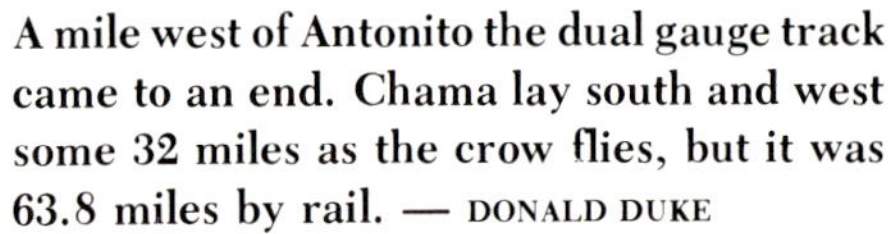
A mile west of Antonito the dual gauge track came to an end. Chama lay south and west some 32 miles as the crow flies, but it was 63.8 miles by rail. — DONALD DUKE

It is downhill most of the way as the eastbound *San Juan* rolls around the big loop at Los Piños tank. It is 5:15 P.M. on the clock and the summer sun is still high. This train will not reach Alamosa for another three hours. — R. H. KINDIG

It is 10:20 A.M. and the *San Juan* has just pulled into Cumbres station "On Time." After a short brake test, this train will be off down around Windy Point and bound for Chama. — R. B. JACKSON

Various scenes aboard the *San Juan*. The parlor car section, the oval illuminated tail sign, the dining table, the chef at work in his clean kitchen, the train crew collecting tickets, and the old oil overhead lamps which stood as a reminder of by-gone days. — ALL DONALD DUKE

The *San Juan* climbing the westside of Cumbres Pass near Coxo. — OTTO PERRY

(BELOW) Against an arid background, the *San Juan* rolls along the New Mexico side of the border at Azotea. — DONALD DUKE

At Carbon Junction the Alamosa-Durango main line is joined by the tracks of the Farmington branch. From this point to Durango the rails follow close to the rushing waters of the Animas River. — DONALD DUKE

The Last San Juan

On January 31, 1951, at 11:30 P.M., narrow-gauge engine No. 488 with its plow covered with snow, pulled 8 Pullman green cars into the Alamosa station, completing the last run. The train had left Durango that morning at 11:15 A.M. behind engine No. 484, which served as the helper engine from Chama to Cumbres. Appropriately, the weather was cold and icy, a fitting farewell to the last daily narrow-gauge passenger train in the 48 states. In the view at the top, the last *San Juan* steams along between Durango and Gato. (RIGHT) The *San Juan* clearing the rails at Cumbres. (BELOW) The last two trains meet at Gato when the clock shows 1:30 P.M., ending 70 years of rail passenger service to the San Juan Basin. — ALL DONALD DUKE

Silverton Branch

With Durango reached and the end of track facilities established, the engineers, graders and trackworkers hurried toward their goal — Silverton. Tracklaying began in October and continued until the middle of December, when heavy snows brought the construction to a standstill. Work was resumed in July, but progress was slowed due to weather conditions, difficult engineering problems, and a delay in rail delivery. The railroad's arrival in Silverton was celebrated on July 4, 1882, although it was six days before the tracks were down, marking completion of the San Juan Extension.

In pushing through the Silverton line, the builders met their greatest challenge in the gorge of the Animas River just north of Rockwood. There the granite cliffs rise perpendicularly from the narrow river course and it was necessary to blast a shelf along the left wall wide enough for roadbed and rails. A single mile of construction cost $100,000, a staggering amount in 1881.

A good portion of the branch follows, crosses and recrosses the river. In the distance of 45.2 miles from Durango to Silverton, the railroad climbs more than a half mile in altitude, from Durango's 6,520 feet to Silverton's 9,300.

Silverton was already a busy mining town when the D&RG arrived. The first setback came in 1893 when silver was demonetized as a currency backing. Fourteen years later, in 1907, a financial panic further crippled the mining industry in such a way that it never recovered. The town was originally called Baker's Park, for Captain Charles Baker, the first prospector in the area. The town was rechristened Silverton by a mine operator who remarked: "we may not have gold here, but we have silver by the ton."

After the panic all daily passenger trains became mixed, and soon it was three times per week, then twice and finally once per week. The scenery and the informal operation attracted tourists. While a few cars of ore were still moving, revenue continued to climb carrying passengers who wished to ride a real steam train. In 1947 the D&RGW began to promote excursions on the mixed and before long they were carrying 12,000 passengers per summer. In the summer of 1955 the railroad took a big step and established daily passenger service beginning in mid-June.

Today the *Silverton* is a Registered Historic Landmark by the National Park Service and a National Civil Engineering Landmark by the American Society of Civil Engineers.

At the right, the northbound *Silverton* approaches the famous "High Line," some 700 feet above the rushing waters of the Animas River. — JOHN KRAUSE

Rio Grande
463

Durango station and the *Silverton* during the train's mixed days. Today the platform is a beehive of activity at train time. Passengers reserve tickets weeks in advance and late-comers cue up at ticket windows for cancellations. (LEFT) A Durango bound *Silverton* approaching the "High Line," a six foot ledge blasted in the face of the sheer rock of the mountain. Although derailments are infrequent, no train has ever gone over the edge of the canyon. (OPPOSITE PAGE) The "High Line" is high and the rails squeeze through on a precarious ledge. From the right-of-way to the river it is a sheer drop of 700 feet. — ALL JOHN KRAUSE

The *Silver Vista* car was one little effort to plug tourism on its narrow-gauge lines. It was built at the Alamosa shops in 1948, and was erected on the frame of an old outfit car. This glass topped observation car was placed in service in June 1948 on the *Silverton*, and was used on excursions. It was destroyed by fire in the same shops on September 30, 1953. In this scene the *Silverton* is steaming along the Animas River bound for Silverton. — DONALD DUKE

Geologists have been fascinated by the Silverton line as giving, along its few miles, a glimpse of several hundred million years' development of the earth's surface. Five miles south of Silverton the train passes through a gorge of the Animas River some 2,000 feet deep, too narrow for more than the railroad and the river. In this scene the *Silverton* may be seen smoking along its tortuous course. — JOHN KRAUSE

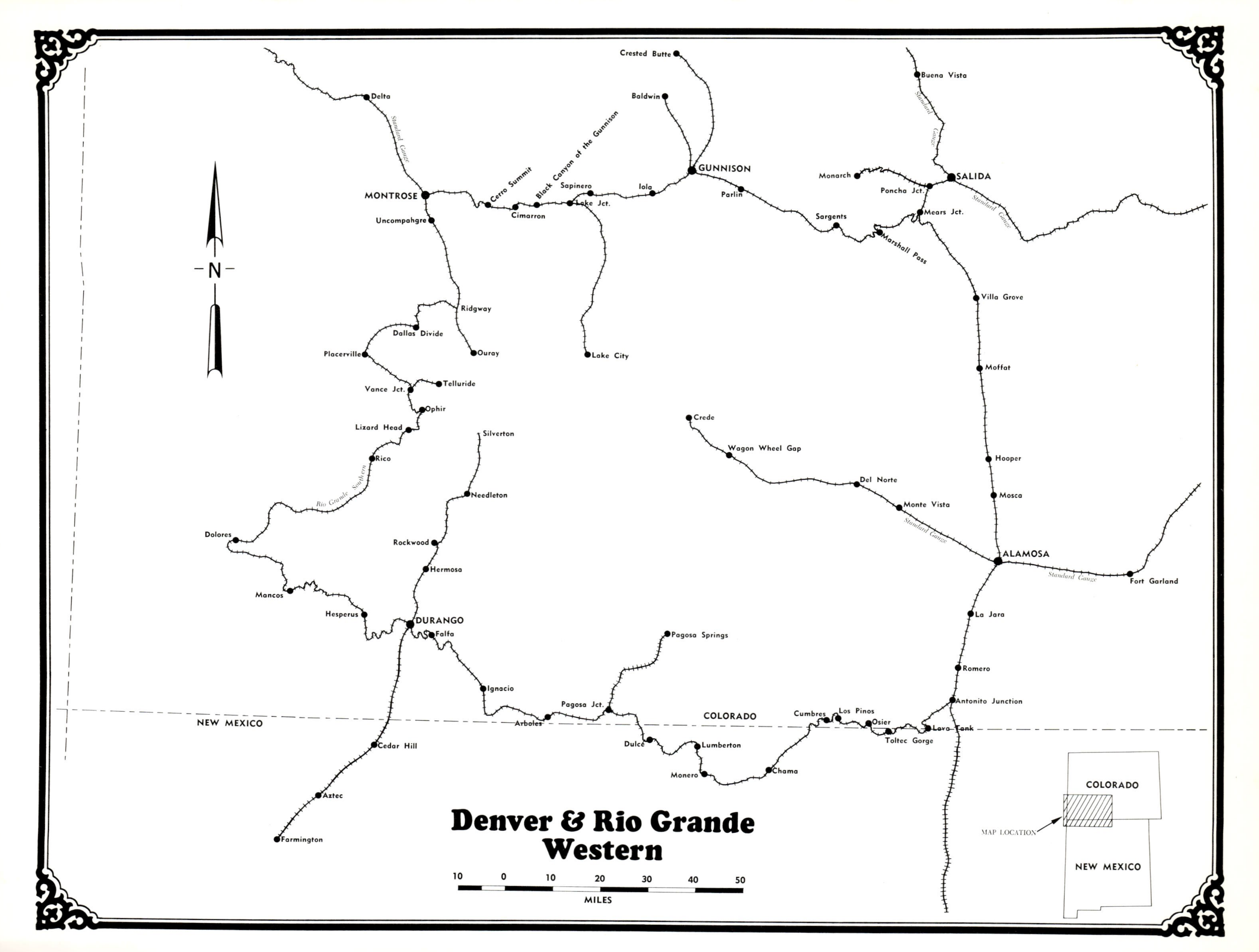

Denver & Rio Grande Western
N
10 0 10 20 30 40 50
MILES
COLORADO
NEW MEXICO
MAP LOCATION
Crested Butte
Baldwin
Delta
Standard Gauge
GUNNISON
Black Canyon of the Gunnison
Cerro Summit
Sapinero
Iola
MONTROSE
Cimarron
Lake Jct.
Parlin
Uncompahgre
Buena Vista
Monarch
SALIDA
Poncha Jct.
Mears Jct.
Sargents
Marshall Pass
Villa Grove
Moffat
Hooper
Mosca
ALAMOSA
Fort Garland
Ridgway
Ouray
Dallas Divide
Placerville
Lake City
Vance Jct.
Telluride
Ophir
Lizard Head
Rico
Rio Grande Southern
Silverton
Needleton
Rockwood
Hermosa
Dolores
Mancos
Hesperus
DURANGO
Falfa
Ignacio
Pagosa Springs
Pagosa Jct.
Arboles
Dulce
Lumberton
Monero
Chama
Cumbres
Los Pinos
Osier
Toltec Gorge
Lava Tank
Antonito Junction
Romero
La Jara
Crede
Wagon Wheel Gap
Del Norte
Monte Vista
Cedar Hill
Aztec
Farmington

No. 463, on the left, has just left Silverton and begins the run back to Durango in mixed train days. (**RIGHT**) The *Silverton* is steaming along the banks of the Animas River with parlor car *Alamosa*. — BOTH JOHN KRAUSE

The photographer risked his neck to get this picture of the *Silverton* headed toward Durango, a few miles out of Silverton. The famous *Silver Vista* brings up the rear. — JOHN KRAUSE

Engine No. 453 switching cars in the Silverton yard before the tourist train became popular. — DONALD DUKE

The *Silverton* at the depot waiting for the trip back to Durango. Today the train runs down to the main street of town so that tourists have more time to spend browsing in the shops. — JOHN KRAUSE

The *Silverton* leaving town behind engine No. 478. Here it crosses a tributary of the Animas River, and heads down into the canyon. Silverton may be seen in the background. (OPPOSITE PAGE) Under a rolling cloud of smoke and cinders, the *Silverton* labors through Rockwood Cut as it steams toward Silverton. — BOTH JOHN KRAUSE

476

Black smoke signals the arrival of the Farmington branch local as it leaves Durango and heads down the line. Note the width of the trestle deck, originally designed for standard gauge trains. — JOHN KRAUSE

Farmington Branch

Today, Farmington, New Mexico, is a giant in oil, gas and uranium. The town was developed in 1879 when William Locke established a fruit industry in the region. It later changed to a cowboy town and was nearly wiped off the map when a drunk cowboy shot an Indian there. The branch was built down the Animas River Valley 48 miles from Carbon Junction in 1905. In anticipation of a standard gauge connection off the Santa Fe or Southern Pacific to the south, the branch was built standard gauge at first and then later converted to narrow-gauge in 1923. (TOP RIGHT) A train load of gas pipe rolls through Aztec, 35 miles south of Durango. — JOHN KRAUSE (CENTER) Farmington station circa 1939. — R. B. JACKSON (BELOW) Mikado No. 488 steaming along the desert-like countryside near Cedar Hill. — DONALD DUKE

Alamosa - Salida Main Line

After the D&RG built a new standard gauge line over La Veta Pass to Alamosa in 1899, the narrow-gauge route between Pueblo and Alamosa was abandoned. Had the road not already extended an existing line running from Mears Junction to Orient via Villa Grove to Alamosa in 1890, the Alamosa-Durango line would have been isolated save for the long connection via the Rio Grande Southern. The first part of this route was built in 1881 to serve the Colorado Fuel & Iron mine at the base of the Sangre de Cristo Mountains, a distance of 28 miles. The 53 mile extension from Villa Grove to Alamosa Junction contained the fifth-longest straight tangent of railroad in the country. The section from Hooper to Alamosa was 3-railed in 1928, In the scene above, No. 494 does a bit of switching at Hooper, 20 miles north of Alamosa. (LEFT) No. 497 at Mears Junction, ready to push a train over Poncha Pass. — BOTH DONALD DUKE

Traffic between Alamosa and Salida via Poncha Pass had been spartan for years. The line had been kept open mainly as a direct connection to avoid loading narrow-gauge rolling stock on standard gauge cars and shipping around the long way. In these scenes of the last run on February 15, 1951, No. 482 easily handles two cars over the line. (TOP LEFT) The last train racing along at Hooper. (CENTER) The same train at Moffat. (LOWER LEFT) No. 182 nearing Round Hill. (BELOW) Crossing the Salida-Gunnison main line at Mears Junction, just 11 miles from Salida. — ALL ROBERT W. RICHARDSON

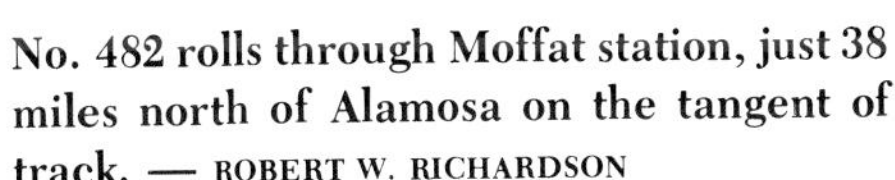

No. 482 rolls through Moffat station, just 38 miles north of Alamosa on the tangent of track. — ROBERT W. RICHARDSON

The successful occupation of the Royal Gorge provided the D&RG with the key to transportation of most of all Colorado's mining products and a route to Salt Lake. The railroad established the town of Salida, north of the gorge, as a division point for its extension West. Here the railroad vaulted the continental divide once again at Marshall Pass (10,860 feet), a grade more gentle than Monarch 10 miles to the north. The rails generally followed Otto Mears toll road which wound up Poncha Creek on the east slope and descended the valley of Tomichi Creek on the west. Service was inaugurated to Sargent, a helper station at the base of Marshall Pass by July 16, 1881, and to Gunnison by August 5, 1881, a mining and farm center. As the rails pushed west from Gunnison in 1882, the tracks followed the Gunnison River into the upper part of the Black Canyon as far as Crystal Creek. Here engineers found construction through the lower canyon impossible due to tight clearances and excessive drop in the river of over 100 feet in one direction. The Gunnison was crossed and the rails followed up the Cimarron Canyon to a natural exit where the town of Cimarron was established as a helper station for Cerro Summit. From here west, the rails were laid up a 4 percent grade to the summit, and then down hill all the way to Montrose. Rails reached there on September 8, 1882, and a trading and fruit growing center was established.

Various branch lines were built off the main line to open up the mineral wealth of the mountain country. A 7 mile line was built from Poncha Junction to Maysville in 1881 to tap the gold and silver mines. It was extended in 1883 to Monarch. To reach Monarch a double hairpin or lariat curve was constructed and a tri-level switchback at Garfield. From Gunnison in 1881, a 29-mile line followed the broad valley of the Gunnison River to Crested Butte, site of coal mines. From Gunnison the D&RG operated the Baldwin branch of the old Colorado & Southern from 1911-1937 and then purchased it. The Baldwin branch originated timothy hay, livestock and coal. In 1887 the railroad extended the 36-mile line south of Montrose to Ouray, site of a rich silver lode. The tracks followed close to the Uncompahgre River over its entire distance.

In the scene at the right, engine No. 480 prepares to enter the west end of the Marshall Pass sheds. The shed was a half mile in length and protected the line from drifts at this summit location. — JOHN KRAUSE

Salida to Montrose

Salida, where the main line met the narrow-gauge. In this scene, a standard gauge switcher races a narrow-gauge engine in the dual gauge yard. The roundhouse and shops were located alongside the coaling tower in the background. — JOHN KRAUSE

The *Shavano*, the Salida-Montrose daily passenger train approaches Mears Junction prior to its ascent of Marshall Pass and the run to Gunnison. — R. H. KINDIG (RIGHT) An empty coal train nears Mear Junction on the Marshall Pass line. — ROBERT W. RICHARDSON

The Sapinero-Salida main line was abandoned in 1955 and then scrapped. In the above scene, No. 489 with a scrap train heads down the east side of Marshall Pass near Gray's. (RIGHT) The same train further down the slopes of Marshall Pass at Shirley Curve. — BOTH JOHN KRAUSE

Marshall Pass Snowsheds

The summit of Marshall Pass was equipped with engine, depot, and boardinghouse facilities, all integrated into a unique twisting snowshed. In the scene above, No. 480 comes charging out of the west end of the shed, running light to become a pusher from Sargent to the Summit. (LEFT) No. 480 on the Marshall Pass turntable within the shed itself. (LOWER LEFT) The scrappers inside the shed in 1955. Note all the light in the roof, showing that a part of the shed roof had already fallen in. — ALL JOHN KRAUSE

A summit bound train coming up the westside of Marshall Pass. From this vantage point at the summit, one can see the train passing Shawano tank and by following the canyon down, one would end up at Sargent. — JOHN KRAUSE

Sargent sat at the western foot of Marshall Pass. This helper station was a sizeable lumber town at one time. The rail facility included a turntable, wye, coaling tower, water tank, eating house, and section house. In this view, No. 489 is about to begin the ascent of Marshall Pass. (BELOW) Engine No. 489 takes on water from the Sargent tank in preparation for the climb to the summit. — BOTH JOHN KRAUSE

Under a rolling cloud of smoke, No. 480 creaks along the grass covered right-of-way at Doyle, 18.9 miles east of Gunnison. — JOHN KRAUSE

Cattle Loading at Parlin

Loading Mexican longhorns at Parlin: the last stock train to ever run over the Marshall Pass line. The rulebook would only permit four engines on a single train when in stock service over Marshall. Two engines brought the train from Gunnison to Parlin. After loading they double-headed to Sargents where two additional locomotives were waiting to cut into the train and head up Marshall Pass. On reaching the summit, one locomotive took the train under control to Salida, while the other three engines ran ahead down the hill separately. — ALL JOHN KRAUSE

Mikado No. 489, its smoke blowing to far horizons, whirls through Parlin with a load of rail scrap during the tearing up of the Gunnison line. — JOHN KRAUSE

Gunnison

The Gunnison roundhouse was built in a semicircle and faced a powered turntable. For years the terminal was teeming with iron horses and the yard was always clear of weeds. In this 1954 scene at the left, engine No. 483 is warming up for a run to Salida. (BELOW) A train of Crested Butte coal leaves Gunnison for the furnaces of the Colorado Fuel & Iron Co. at Pueblo. — BOTH JOHN KRAUSE

Locomotive No. 268 was painted orange and silver with black striping for the Chicago Railroad Fair. On its return to Gunnison it retained its fancy livery. A short train is shown here arriving at Sapinero, a lumber and trout fishing resort town named after a Ute Indian chief. — JOHN KRAUSE

Following completion of the branch to Crested Butte, the main line was extended west along the banks of the Gunnison River to Sapinero, a distance of 25.6 miles. Originally called Soap Creek, the name was changed to honor another Ute Indian chief. The station became a shipping point for lumber, livestock, and agricultural products. In the scene above, No. 268 has left Sapinero a few minutes earlier with a load of stock. (RIGHT) The same train working its way along the river toward Gunnison. (BELOW) Heading back to Gunnison. — ALL JOHN KRAUSE

A stock train steaming through Iola, 10 miles west of Gunnison. At one time this roadside town was a stock shipping point. — JOHN KRAUSE

The last train to leave Sapinero for Gunnison was this gathering of old cars on a September day in 1954. The rails were pulled up the following year. — JOHN KRAUSE

Locomotive No. 361 on the point of a westbound freight at Curecanti Needle. A brakeman releases the brakes on a cut of cars to be picked up. (LEFT) A freight emerges from the Canyon of Cimarron via the Cimarron River close to the town of Cimarron. — BOTH R. H. KINDIG

Black Canyon of the Gunnison

By the end of August 1882, the road was in full operation from Gunnison through the Black Canyon, to Cimarron. The last mile of track in the canyon was said to have cost more than the entire construction through the Royal Gorge. The Black Canyon became a major tourist attraction, especially the Curecanti Needle, a rock pinnacle in the depths of the canyon. The needle became the symbol and insigne of the railroad for years. The line through the canyon was a vital link between the booming San Juan country and the lines to Leadville and Pueblo. After completion of the standard gauge line to Salt Lake via Tennessee Pass, the original Marshall Pass line was relegated to secondary status. Dismantling of the line through the canyon in 1949 between Sapinero and Cedar Creek (below Cerro Summit) broke the "narrow-gauge circle." This isolated the Ouray branch, and it severed the original narrow-gauge route between Denver and Salt Lake. (BELOW) Rocky Mountain Railroad Club excursion in the Black Canyon in September 1948. — DONALD DUKE

Cerro Summit

Cimarron was established as a helper station to assist trains up the 4 percent grade to a spot called Cerro Summit. From an elevation of 6,831 feet at Cimarron, the rails climbed 7,968 feet in a little over 7 miles. From the summit is was downhill all the way to Montrose at 5,811 feet. Cerro hill caused nothing but trouble over the years, and eventually was the principle cause for abandonment of most of the Montrose-Sapinero segment in 1949. (ABOVE) No. 361 on Cerro in 1946. — JOHN MAXWELL (RIGHT) No. 454 heading up to the summit of Cerro with short train. (LOWER RIGHT) The same train coasting down the west side of the grade. — BOTH R. H. KINDIG

Ouray Branch

Ouray lies pocketed in a pear-shaped valley surrounded by lofty peaks of the San Juan Range. Founded in 1875 when rich silver lodes were discovered locally, the area boomed through the 1880's until devaluation of silver. Gold was discovered in 1896 followed by lead and zinc. A 36-mile branch was extended from Montrose south to Ouray in 1887 to serve the mines. With the dismantling of the Rio Grande Southern in 1953 the Ouray section was taken-up and the Montrose-Ridgway portion of the branch converted to standard gauge. (LEFT) Narrow-gauge enginehouse at Montrose and line up of Ouray branch power. — DONALD DUKE (BELOW) Ridgway bound stock extra, just minutes out of Montrose. — JOHN KRAUSE

318
Rio Grande
318

When the Cerro Summit section of the Montrose-Salida line was scrapped this isolated the Ouray branch. The only narrow-gauge connection was via the RGS. (RIGHT) The D&RG 450 class called "Mudhens" were too heavy for the Ridgway-Ouray section of the branch. No. 318 is shown on the trestle approaching Ouray. (BELOW) Stock loading at Ridgway. (OPPOSITE PAGE) A train of coal steams south of Montrose with black diamonds for Ridgway and Ouray. — ALL JOHN KRAUSE

483

Crested Butte Branch

The growth of precious metal mining in the western slope of Colorado led to the discovery of coal. Pioneer miners drove their wagons to outcroppings and shoveled enough free coal to supply small smelters. In the newly opened Gunnison country there were reports of large deposits of coal. The arrival of the D&RG provided a natural alliance for transportation and rapid corporate control of large acreages of coal land. The D&RG became active in opening mines along their rights-of-way. Most of what was mined was bituminous coal; the only developed anthracite mines were in the Crested Butte area. Closely associated with coal came the manufacturing of iron and steel. In 1880 the Colorado Coal & Iron Company (later Colorado Fuel & Iron, a part of the Rockefeller empire) was established at Pueblo. Mines were bought from the D&RG and operated as wholly owned facilities with tightly controlled company towns and employees tied to the company store. Coal production peaked during and after World War I and Colorado became the largest steel center and coal producing state west of the Mississippi.

As Crested Butte developed as a coal mining community the D&RG ran a 29-mile line to the region in 1882. The branch was extended to Anthracite, a distance of 4 miles in 1882. In 1893 the narrow gauge tracks were pushed up Kebler Pass to Floresta, 11 additional miles.

Coal mines provided the CF&I with the bulk of coaking coal for years. For an unknown reason the Crested Butte mine was closed in June 1952, thus forcing the abandonment of the Crested Butte branch the same year.

At the left, No. 483 covers the countryside with coal smoke as it works a mixed stock and coal drag along the banks of the Gunnison River at Almont. — JOHN KRAUSE

Rolling north out of Gunnison, the Crested Butte line passes through rich grazing land. In the above scene, three cows impede the passage of a short train. — JOHN KRAUSE **(LEFT) No. 487 blasts an empty coal train out of Almont Canyon en route to Crested Butte. —** DONALD DUKE **(LOWER LEFT) Taking water at Jack's Cabin. (BELOW) The Crested Butte depot, an old time "chick sales," and No. 483 doing a bit of switching. —** BOTH JOHN KRAUSE

A short train of ore leaves the lonely outskirts of Crested Butte for Gunnison. The town was named for the neighboring sharp rocky butte to which fir and pine trees clung precariously. — JOHN KRAUSE

Winter was never a lamb in the valley of the Gunnison River, the reason why Crested Butte became such a successful ski region today. In the scene above, a train of emties leaves Gunnison for the Buttes. (TOP RIGHT) The same train flanging its way past Almont. (RIGHT) Switching loads, empties, and snow at Crested Butte. — ALL ROBERT W. RICHARDSON

Baldwin Branch

The Denver, South Park & Pacific arrived in Gunnison nearly a year after the D&RG. Yet Gunnison was not to be their end of track. The rails were extended 16 miles north to the local coal fields of Castleton and Baldwin the following year, but with the mining boom over in Colorado, plans to build over Ohio Pass en route to Utah were abandoned. The line to Baldwin was entirely disconnected when the Alpine Tunnel line was closed in 1910 and arrangements were made with the D&RG to operate the branch. The line was eventually sold by the Colorado & Southern to the D&RGW in 1937. The stem to Baldwin was removed in 1946 and the complete branch in 1955. (RIGHT) Engine No. 278 at Dolland was photographed with a train of coal from the mine at Castleton. — DONALD DUKE (CENTER) Plow and No. 268 doing a bit of snow removal on the branch. — ROBERT W. RICHARDSON (BELOW) While scrapping the Baldwin branch, No. 268 passes the old Gunnison South Park depot. — JOHN KRAUSE

Monarch Branch

As the main line over Marshall Pass was under construction in 1881, the D&RG could not ignore the booming mining camps of Maysville, Garfield, and Monarch. The branch took off from Poncha Junction and ran 15.3 miles up a canyon with grades of 3.8 percent, and worse. The mountain valley rose so steeply that some outstanding engineering features were utilized. Just west of Maysville, a lariat loop was built which sent the rails the same way they came while climbing the mountain wall. A second loop sent them back toward Monarch. Sheer mountain walls at Garfield prevented loops, so switchbacks raised the rails to Monarch, an elevation of 10,028 feet and just below Monarch Pass. Despite lariat loops and switchbacks, the ruling grade between Maysville and Monarch was 4.5 percent.

The mines played out by World War I time, but the best years were ahead. The Colorado Fuel & Iron bought the mountains to mine limestone for steelmaking. A guaranteed 1,400 tons of rock per day assured the branch a fruitful life, even today. With the abandonment of the narrow-gauge lines west of Salida, the Monarch branch became an isolated stub. In 1956 the line was standard gauged, ending all narrow-gauge operations north of Alamosa.

Heading up to Monarch with a train of empties. The second locomotive is not in sight as this limestone special nears Maysville. — JOHN KRAUSE

The heavier 490 class locomotives were transferred to the Alamosa-Durango line prior to the cut in the Salida-Alamosa segment in 1951. The 480 class engines proved adequate to handle the Monarch service and two engines handled each train. In the scene above, No. 482 charges the grade to Monarch just below the first loop. (LEFT) No. 489 pushes at the rear near the switchback. The Monarch Pass highway is below the locomotive. — BOTH JOHN KRAUSE

At Maysville half of a 52-car train is taken up the hill by both engines out of respect to the grade and the car limit on the switchbacks. In this scene, the lariat loop near Maysville as the first section smokes its way toward the switchbacks. (LEFT) Watching the switchback operation was a sight to behold. Here No. 483 shoves the first half of the train up the switchback while No. 489 is moving up the second cut of the 52-car train. — BOTH JOHN KRAUSE

Delivering empties and picking up loads took a bit of maneuvering at Monarch. In this scene, No. 481 shoves a string of empties upgrade and does the switching while No. 480 waits for clearance to move to the wye. — JOHN KRAUSE

No. 481, shown above, leaves the mine with a train of limestone and heads for the wye. — JOHN KRAUSE (RIGHT) After No. 481 turns on the wye, she takes off for the switchbacks. — PHIL HASTINGS

The climb down the tri-level switchback with loads had to be taken slowly. In the scene at the far left, No. 481 makes its way to the first switch. The brakeman has run ahead and waits by the switchstand. (CENTER) No. 481 pulling ahead with the first section . (RIGHT) No. 481 is backing down the switchback and No. 482 helps brake the section then returns to the second cut. — ALL JOHN KRAUSE

A train of limestone enters the main line at Poncha Junction en route to Salida and the barrel dumper which transfers stone from narrow-gauge cars to standard gauge gondolas. The Gunnison main line is the track straight ahead, but shows little use when this picture was taken. — JOHN KRAUSE

Rio Grande Southern No. 20 at the Colorado Railroad Museum. — DONALD DUKE

5

Rio Grande Southern

The coming of the railroad into the San Juan Mountains of Colorado found Otto Mears better conditioned for the acceptance of this new form of transportation than any of his local contemporaries, including General William J. Palmer, president of the Denver & Rio Grande. The transition from wagon road builder and toll road operator of the San Juan to master builder of narrow-gauge railroads was an easy one.

Otto Mears came to America from Russia at the age of 10, drifted to the Pacific Coast during the gold rush and served in the First Regiment of California Volunteers. He later moved to Colorado Territory where he had a job as storekeeper. It was here he got the idea of going into the toll road business. He saw wagon trains and prospectors moving into the mountains and figured there would be more coming and they could use roads. He later became the foremost toll road builder, operator and packmaster in Colorado. Between 1867 and 1886, Mears constructed a full dozen major wagon roads into the western slope of Colorado. Nearly all of these roads were between mining camps and were mushrooming with traffic as prospectors moved into the mountain country. In a few short years his roads would become the future rights of way for narrow-gauge railroads.

In addition to his road building, Mears was involved in every angle of freighting, maintaining stage service, contracting for mails and delivering supplies to the remotest and most inaccessible claim. His familiarity with transportation and service made him a candidate as railroad builder. In 1882 the Denver & Rio Grande had just arrived in Silverton after building up the spectacular Canyon of the Animas River from Durango. The railroad engineers took a look at the formidable peaks of the Uncompahgre surrounding every side except the pass to which the river vented and decided they had gone far enough! At this time they were also building a line from Montrose south to Ouray. At every point it seemed like Mears' toll roads were being graded for rails. Ouray and Telluride were booming and if the Rio Grande would not build a route to these points out of Silverton, he, Otto Mears, would show them how. After all, it was only 26 miles in distance between Silverton and Ouray.

Ironically, the Rio Grande Southern came into being because of the haste with which Colorado narrow-gauge railroads were surveyed and built. Mears built his Silverton Railroad up Mineral Creek to tap the rich mines in the Red Mountain region. He hoped within a few months to be operating his railroad through the tortuous confines of Uncompahgre Canyon and drop down into Ouray, thus completing the gap. His locating crews were working on Red Mountain trying to find and survey a possible route, but when only 12 miles separated Silverton from Ouray, Mears' surveyors told him he was attempting the impossible. No railroad could ever be put through the canyon on a 7.5 percent grade unless it was a cable or rack line. If Ouray could not be achieved by an extension of the Silverton Railroad, then it could be reached by a gigantic loop railroad around the mountains 162 miles in length. That was how the Rio Grande Southern took form.

Frustrated, Mears sent his surveyors into the field. From its beginning in Durango, his proposed railroad would sweep west to Mancos and Dolores and then head north again via the vast mining operations of Rico, Ophir and Telluride, up the canyon of San Miguel and across Dallas Divide to Ridgway to a connection with the D&RG branch to Ouray. Within this 162 mile run to cover the 12 miles between Red Mountain and Ouray, there were enough mines to make any railroad rich. So it would take some engineering, a lot of loops, snowsheds and spidery trestles and $9,000,000 to complete in 1890 dollars. He would show the Uncompahgre Mountains that it didn't pay to play with Otto Mears.

The Rio Grande Southern Railway was organized in 1889 and a separate corporation called the Rio Grande Southern Construction Company to build the line. Construction began at both ends of the line at the same time and Mears was eager to complete the railroad as quickly as possible in order to tap the fabulously rich discoveries at Placerville, Ophir and Rico which were all awaiting more efficient transportation. The northern end of the line from Ridgway to Telluride, which ran over Dallas Divide, followed closely on an already existing Mears toll road. This somewhat simplified surveying and grading over this portion of the new railroad. The road was built and later operated as two separate sections: the northern running from Ridgway to Rico, and the southern from Durango to Rico. Shortly after construction began out of Durango, the line reached the Porter Coal Mine and the RGS was provided with some immediate revenue.

After passing Lizard Head, construction moved along at a much faster pace. There were fewer trestles to build and much less rock to move. The advancing ends of track from the north and south finally met in December 1891 just 11 miles south of Rico. Although the road was now completed, it had been in business for nearly a year. Scheduled trains had been running between Telluride and Ridgway. The first through train made it over the line in two days, stopping overnight at Rico. Thereafter sleeper service was inaugurated over the line and whisky salesmen, miners and drummers of all kinds made the regular stops.

While the RGS was an immediate success, hauling coal on its southern end and mine supplies, cattle and ore on its northern end, it had no sooner completed its entire length when hard times approached. The demoniterization of silver in 1893 plunged the entire West into panic. Carloadings dropped to only a few cars per day at Telluride and Rico. The Denver & Rio Grande was appointed receiver for the Rio Grande Southern when the road could not make its bond payment.

From that day on the Rio Grande Southern was relegated to minority status and used as a repository for all the D&RG's woes and cast off equipment. Naturally the road was charged huge sums for joint use of terminals and roundhouse space, leased locomotives, and the fee for rolling stock repair often equaled the price of a new car. With 70 percent of the Southern's stock in its back pocket, the D&RG simply looted the treasury. One can only speculate as to why the RGS became such a stepchild and was not absorbed into the D&RG system since it was the originator of considerable traffic. One reason might be the top-heavy executive payroll lined with Rio Grande management? After all, the D&RG was eventually going to get the traffic as a secondary carrier!

For no good reason at all the Rio Grande Southern chugged down through the years, its freight trains replacing the vanishing carloadings of ore with sheep, lumber, cattle, and agricultural products. The tourists and mine owners who frequented the region found that the daily passenger run in each direction had given way to a train three times a week and many times this became a mixed train when there was not sufficient traffic to justify a full freight run that day.

While trains were cut back to the bone, the easiest way to save money was to defer track maintenance. Although the Southern's right-of-way was in a heavy precipitation zone during the winter season, and rivers rose in the spring and took its tracks down river with regularity, little was done in the way of preventive care. If a landslide or a snowslide blocked the track, the RGS just built around it. Bridges were replaced with little support even though they were repeatedly torn out. The only trestles built like the Rock of Gibralter were those at Ophir. Parent Rio Grande repeatedly grasped at the chance to abandon the road when it was closed down due to a disaster, but embattered communities and counties along the line could not lose their entire contact with the outside world and fought with gusto to save the RGS in the State legislature.

Accidents were frequent on the RGS on account of the rough and uneven track. An engineer is said to have remarked, "We never know if we are on the rails or on the ground, the engines ride so rough. If the engine comes to a complete halt, we know we are on the ground and just jack 'er up and she is back on the track." On a makeshift railroad running over incredible heights and above abysmal crevasses, the incidence of disaster was measureably higher than on most narrow-gauge railroads. A couple of trains went through trestles at Ophir and Lightner Creek. A light engine went through the trestle at Bilk Creek, just below Vance Junction, and a train following piled on top of her 15 minutes later because someone failed to send back a flagman. Minor derailments were so commonplace that the dispatcher at Durango knew for sure when a train was more than half a day late that the crew were out somewhere re-railing a car or locomotive. There were telephones all along the line and at unattended stations, but they seldom worked. Crews made it a practice to always carry emergency rations along in their cabooses for at least two days.

The United States Railroad Administration took over the RGS during World War I and some improvements were made to the physical plant. While other railroads were making profits the RGS continued to turn in six figure losses. By 1924 the operation ratio reached 125 percent, a national record for the time. The prosperity of the "Roaring Twenties" never touched the RGS and its accumulated deficits headed for the $3-million dollar mark. During December 1929, while every railroad was handing out extra dividend checks, the RGS went into receivership under Victor A. Miller, a Denver attorney. To make matters worse the last operating mine of consequence at Pandora was closed and the Ames slide near Ophir closed the line for weeks, costing the RGS its through traffic and seasonal livestock shipments.

Freed from the Denver & Rio Grande Western "yoke," Victor Miller set about the reduction of operating costs and to this end he abandoned steam passenger service and substituted it with seven motorized rail cars which subsequently became known as *Galloping Geese*. These huge silver painted rail vans had for their power Winton and Pierce Arrow motors, a large l.c.l. compartment in the rear and seats for six passengers in the forward section with the driver. The depression cost the RGS approximately 85 percent of its profits and Miller received permission to suspend all property taxes along the line as a means to keep the road running. He presented a new plan for reorganization to the court and was refused. He quickly resigned. Cass M. Herrington, another Denver attorney was appointed receiver. Herrington's regime, terminated by his death in 1948, was marked by further loss of business. After Herrington applied for abandonment of the line in 1941, local citizens took up the right to save the road and went to the Reconstruction Finance Corporation for a loan. The following year the Defense Supplies Corporation bought the road's equipment and leased it back. The Office of Defense Transportation requisitioned the entire line, but withdrew upon objection from the Defense Supplies Corp. Another Federal loan was obtained in 1945, but the RGS was too far gone to survive much longer. *Galloping Goose* service between Durango and Dolores was cut in 1941, and all passenger, mail, and l.c.l. carried in highway trucks.

Pierpont Fuller, Jr., succeeded Herrington as receiver and served the road until the very end. The last sources of traffic were being diverted to trucks, and in 1948 the mill of the Montezuma Lumber Company near Dolores burned to the ground, thus ending a prime source of revenue. During 1948 passenger service via *Galloping Goose* was discontinued between Ridgway and Dolores and the mail was handled by highway trucks. By this time rail buffs flocked to see the RGS before she was scrapped. In 1950 someone got the idea of cutting a window in the freight compartment of the *Geese* and thereby haul more tourists. *Geese* Nos. 3 to 5 and 7 were modified to seat passengers in this section with old Denver streetcar seats. These tourist-rail-motor cars operated during the summer months taking tourists from Ridgway to Lizard Head, and from Durango to Dolores. They were also available for charter anytime with advance notice.

Hard times continued to plague the RGS as always. During the winter of 1948-49 for instance, Rotary 2 blew up at Vance Junction. Once the line was open zinc prices fell and the Rico-American Mine closed for good, and then melting snow took out the line between Rico and Dolores. It was things just like this that continued to plague the road. Year after year it happened and with the debt growing at $8,000 per month there was little left to justify further operations. Judge William Lee Knous granted permission to suspend all operations effective December 17, 1951.

There were several "last runs" in September to accommodate all the rail enthusiasts who had been so faithful to the Rio Grande Southern over the years. On November 15, 1951, engine No. 20 made a series of three-day trips between Durango and Rico. Finally locomotive No. 461 was sent out to collect all the cars on the line and deliver them to the D&RGW. The final Rio Grande Southern train was run on December 27, 1951, when No. 464 brought the last cars in from Mancos. The fire in the boiler was dropped and the long struggle was at last over! The Interstate Commerce Commission finally granted Receiver J. Pierpont Fuller's application to abandon the railroad on April 15, 1952 — the Rio Grande Southern was dead for all time.

464
Rio Grande

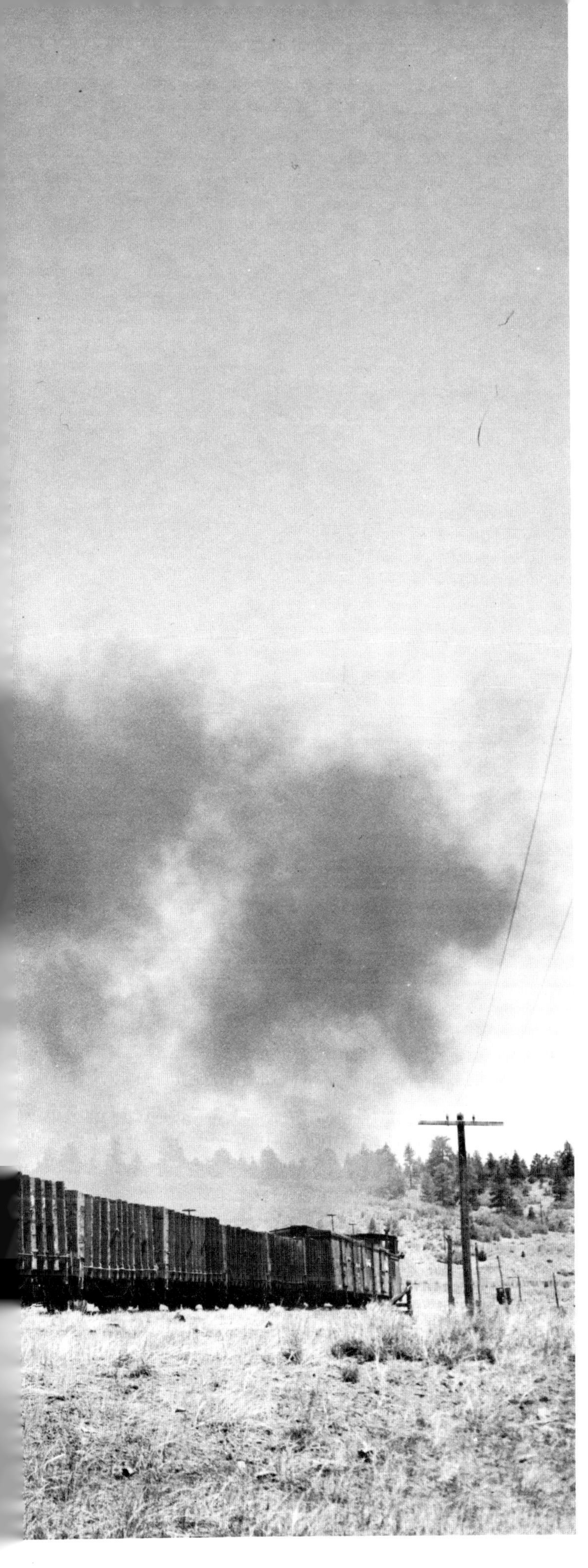

Deep in the heart of the La Plata Mountain country, No. 464 steams toward Hesperus, a farm village and at one time a large agricultural, livestock and coal shipping point. — JOHN KRAUSE

Mancos became a jumping off place for miners and prospectors bound for the La Plata Mountains, once noted for their silver lodes. Much mining was done above timberline, lending support to the old prospectors' maxim: "A good silver mine is above timberline ten times out of nine." In the above scene, leased No. 452 leaves Mancos station with 19 cars with the assist of No. 20 at the rear. — R. H. KINDIG (LEFT) Dolores, in the heart of the mine and grazing district, periodically lives and dies with the mining and cattle industry. At one time it was a timber shipping center, and during its final years Dolores was a bean dispatch point. In this scene are three engines, No. 319 is on a rail excursion, No. 452 is waiting for a freight and No. 20 is out of service — JOHN KRAUSE (LOWER) An interesting three-way stub switch located at the north end of the Dolores yard. — PHIL RONFOR

Stoner was a post office, flag station, water tank, and Ranger Station all comprised into one. Stoner was located midway between Dolores and Rico. In the above scene, No. 319 pauses alongside the Stoner tank while the engineer is checking the crosshead. — PHIL RONFOR (LEFT) Rico, once a gold, silver, lead and zinc mining region became Colorado's last outpost of the old West with its false-front framed buildings. Here No. 20 pauses alongside the depot overlooking the mines. — ROBERT W. RICHARDSON

Lizard Head Pass at 10,250 feet elevation, was the highest point on the Rio Grande Southern. At the top of the pass the "wye" was covered for almost a quarter mile by a frame shed, built to keep snow from blocking the tracks. Snowfall at this point is extremely heavy. Lizard Head was also a favorite location for photographers. In the above scene, No. 319 poses with an excursion train. (LEFT) A Rocky Mountain Railway Club train at the same location with engine No. 20. — BOTH PHIL RONFOR

The Ophir-Trout Lake-Lizard Head region of Colorado contained the most spectacular sections of railroading in the West. (LEFT) The original Goose No. 3 has just crossed Trout Lake trestle during the winter of 1945. — ROBERT W. RICHARDSON (LOWER LEFT) No. 4 on the upper Ophir trestles. — DONALD DUKE (BELOW) Rebuilt Goose No. 3 at Ophir station in 1947. — RICHARD B. JACKSON (LOWER RIGHT) Goose No. 3 leaving Lizard Head sheds. — RICHARD W. RICHARDSON

No. 461 rolls across the lower part of the horseshoe at Ophir with the station at the far left. North of Ophir are the Ophir Needles, huge masses of gray granite that dominate the landscape. — JOHN KRAUSE

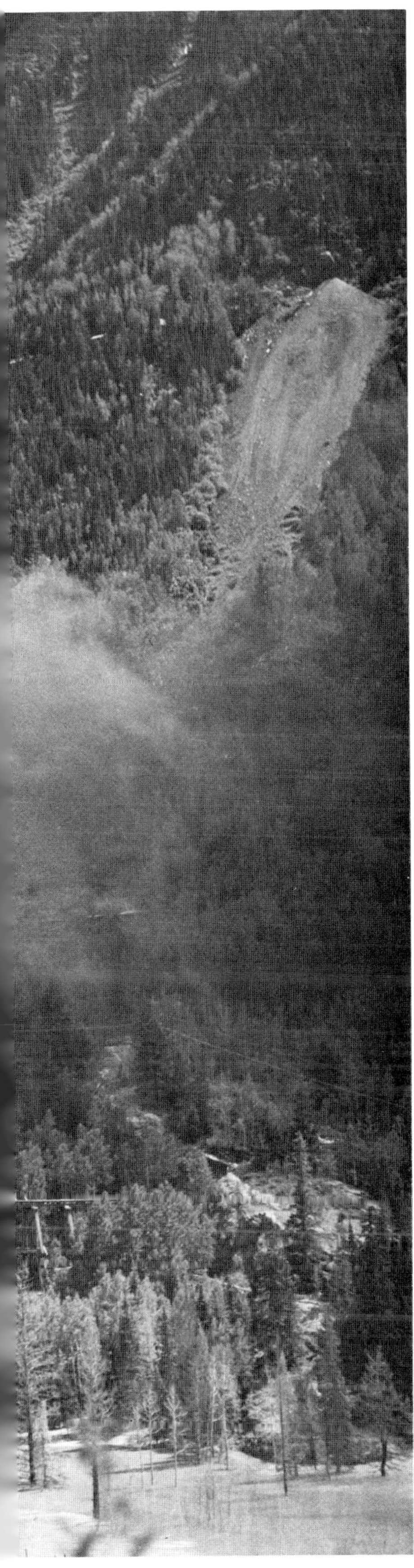

Ophir Loop was one of the remarkable engineering feats in the construction of the RGS. In order to route the railroad past Ophir and eliminate excessive grades, the tracks were laid in the shape of a great horseshoe, a section of which is supported on high wooden trestles. In their course the rails almost overlap themselves. (ABOVE) No. 461 rolls past Ophir station. (BELOW LEFT) Heading out of Ophir for Lizard Head. (BELOW RIGHT) On the upper Ophir trestles in winter. — ROBERT W. RICHARDSON

Leaving Ophir for Lizard Head with No. 74. — PHIL RONFOR

Placerville was originally a placer mining camp. When the mines played out, it became a center for cattle and sheep. In the above scene a freight heads toward Placerville located along the rushing San Miguel River. — JOHN KRAUSE (RIGHT) No. 74 doing a bit of switching at Placerville. — PHIL RONFOR

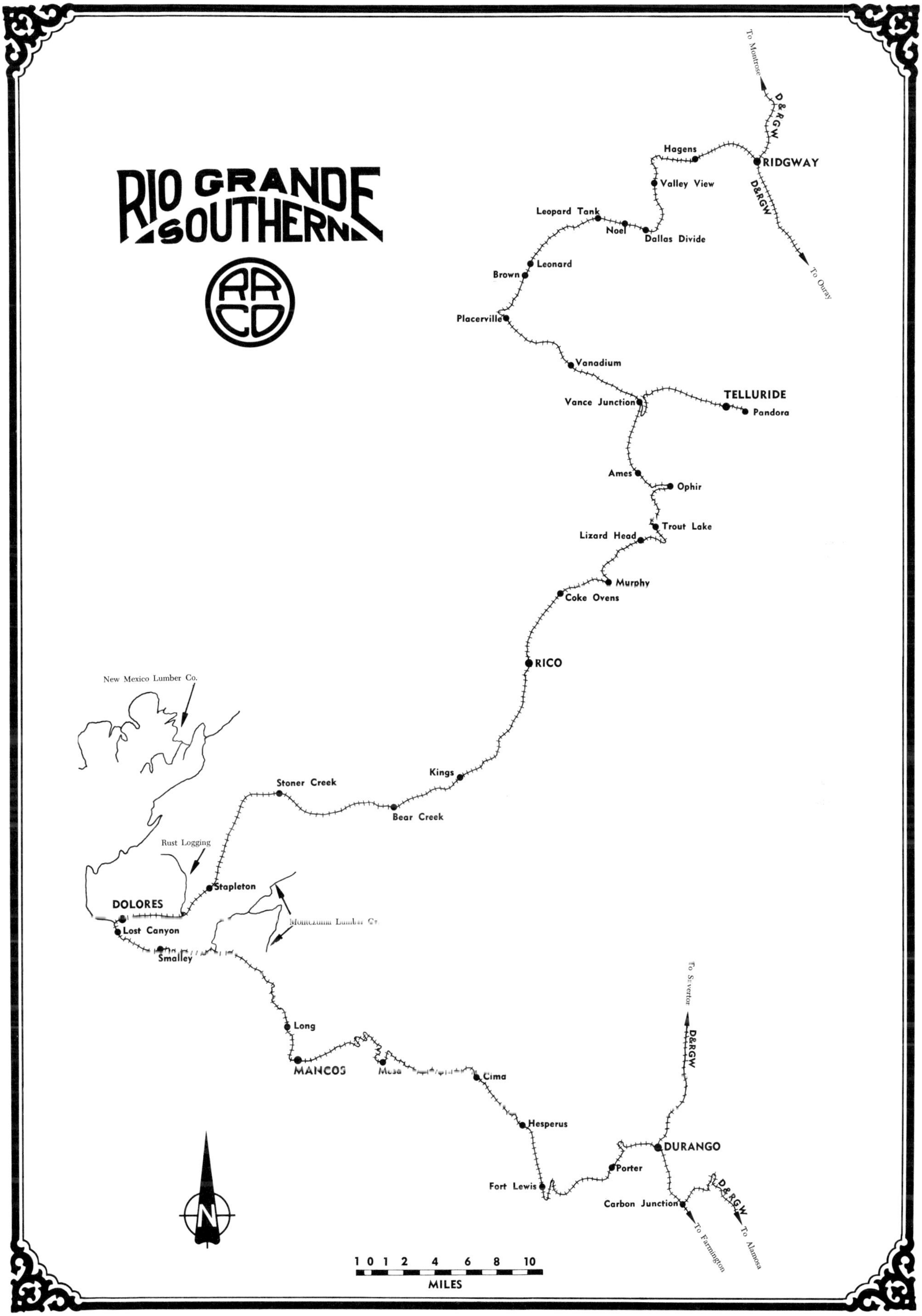

RIO GRANDE SOUTHERN

To Montrose
D&RGW
Hagens
RIDGWAY
D&RGW
Valley View
Leopard Tank
Noel
Dallas Divide
To Ouray
Leonard
Brown
Placerville
Vanadium
Vance Junction
TELLURIDE
Pandora
Ames
Ophir
Trout Lake
Lizard Head
Murphy
Coke Ovens
RICO
New Mexico Lumber Co.
Kings
Stoner Creek
Bear Creek
Rust Logging
Stapleton
DOLORES
Lost Canyon
Montezuma Lumber Co.
Smalley
To Silverton
Long
D&RGW
MANCOS
Mesa
Cima
Hesperus
DURANGO
Porter
Fort Lewis
D&RGW
Carbon Junction
To Farmington
To Alamosa
N
1 0 1 2 4 6 8 10
MILES

Rich veins of silver, assaying at $1,200 a ton, caused a rush to Telluride in 1875. Soon the surrounding mountainsides were pitted with prospect holes. Telluride enjoyed a wild prosperity as new veins were uncovered. It was little wonder the Rio Grande Southern build a branch from Vance Junction to Telluride in 1890. At the peak of the boom, the Smuggler Mine at Pandora, two miles east of Telluride, became world famous for the richness of its lode. (LEFT) An excursion train leaves Vance Junction for Telluride with engine No. 74 on the head end. — OTTO PERRY. (BELOW) No. 74 at the Smuggler Mine headquarters at Pandora in 1949. The actual mine is located on the mountain shoulder at the end of the zigzag in the background. — PHIL RONFOR

At the height of the stock rush of 1951, Robert W. Richardson was on hand with his camera and found No. 74 at Placerville switching stock cars just outside the yard limits.

The San Miguel River Canyon, its red walls formed of intricately eroded strata, echoes an No. 462 makes the curve to Placerville, and wheel flanges on the stock cars sing as they follow the locomotive along the slim gauge rails. — R. H. KINDIG

Scrap dealer Hyman-Michaels purchased the Rio Grande Southern for $409,000 and turned around and sold their interest to two other firms. No. 461 and various outfit cars were used in the scrapping operation. (ABOVE) The scrap train pulls into Brown water tank en route to Placerville. (LEFT) Crossing Leopard Creek near Brown. (OPPOSITE PAGE) Scrap train rolling down the west side of Dallas Divide at Noel. — ALL JOHN KRAUSE

Dallas Divide, located 13 miles west of Ridgway, by rail, is situated on the crest of the Uncompahgre Plateau, its higher regions covered with dense forests interspersed with sage flats. To the south rise the forbidding La Plata Range, with many summits reaching 14,000 feet or more. In this scene, No. 461 rolls down the westside of Dallas Divide and glides across Dead Horse Canyon at Wade with a stock extra. — ROBERT W. RICHARDSON

Denver & Rio Grande Western No. 464 on lease to the RGS heads down grade at Peak, trailing a mixed ore, stock, and lumber train. In the background the imposing Uncompahgre Range, soon to be covered with a mass of snow as winter sets in. — ROBERT W. RICHARDSON

No. 461 rolls down Dallas Divide grade at Valley View. In this scene the magnificent Uncompahgre Range blends with the grass covered slopes of the plateau. Before long the quaking aspens, nipped by frost, will change the foliage from green to yellow and red. — JOHN KRAUSE

At Ridgway, the Uncompahgre Mountains are over-shadowed by the smoke-blackened, red brick shops of the RGS. A scattering of frame cottages along a few rutted streets form this agricultural and livestock shipping point, and northern terminus of the line. (ABOVE) The scrap train leaves Ridgway and heads up Dallas Divide. (RIGHT) A short train at Ridgway. — BOTH JOHN KRAUSE

On November 15, 1951, the RGS began the last runs, taking a bunch of cars to Durango from the soon to be isolated Montrose-Ouray line of the D&RGW. (RIGHT) No. 461 leaving the Ridgway shops ladder track for the depot down the main line. (CENTER) While gathering cars, No. 461 pulls alongside the D&RGW Ridgway depot. — BOTH ROBERT W RICHARDSON

Galloping Goose No. 3 at the Ridgway station in 1940. — R. H. KINDIG

Ridgway was named in honor of Robert M. Ridgway, the man in charge of construction of the line from here to Rico. At the same time Ridgway was also the first superintendent of the road, jointly with his position as superintendent of the 3rd division of the D&RG. He located the company shops at the northern end of the line. In these scenes, No. 452 at the water tank close to the shop building. — BOTH ROBERT W. RICHARDSON

Locomotive No. 74 was built by the Brooks Locomotive Works in 1898 for the Colorado & Northwestern which later became a part of the Colorado & Southern. When the C&S changed the gauge on its Leadville-Climax branch from narrow to standard the engine was sold to a scrap dealer. The old engine was purchased by the RGS in 1948, but was not popular with crews as she was hard to steam. (BELOW) No. 455 came to the RGS in 1939 from the D&RGW and was the first engine to be painted with the new Rio Grande Southern herald. — BOTH DONALD DUKE

No. 461 dusts off the fresh snow from the rails as she works the last load of Rico ore upgrade past Coke Ovens. (BELOW) Two freight trains gather together and pull into Placerville. — BOTH ROBERT W. WICHARDSON

Nos. 461 and 464 cross the big trestles at Ophir during November 1951. — ROBERT W. RICHARDSON

No. 464 prepares to take on water during a snowstorm at Durango. This was one of the last Rio Grande Southern trains to leave Durango for Ridgway on December 1951. — ROBERT W. RICHARDSON

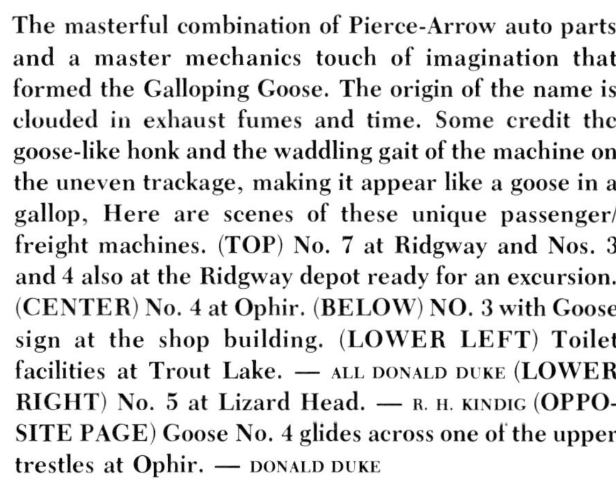

The masterful combination of Pierce-Arrow auto parts and a master mechanics touch of imagination that formed the Galloping Goose. The origin of the name is clouded in exhaust fumes and time. Some credit the goose-like honk and the waddling gait of the machine on the uneven trackage, making it appear like a goose in a gallop, Here are scenes of these unique passenger/freight machines. (TOP) No. 7 at Ridgway and Nos. 3 and 4 also at the Ridgway depot ready for an excursion. (CENTER) No. 4 at Ophir. (BELOW) NO. 3 with Goose sign at the shop building. (LOWER LEFT) Toilet facilities at Trout Lake. — ALL DONALD DUKE (LOWER RIGHT) No. 5 at Lizard Head. — R. H. KINDIG (OPPOSITE PAGE) Goose No. 4 glides across one of the upper trestles at Ophir. — DONALD DUKE

6

Southern Pacific

The Southern Pacific's Keeler Branch was the last common carrier narrow-gauge west of the Rocky Mountains in the old 48 states. For 70 rail miles the vestige of the old Carson & Colorado followed along the east side of the Owens Valley between Keeler and Laws. The route was shadowed on the west by Mount Whitney, highest peak in the United States and on the east by Death Valley, lowest and hottest spot in the country.

The Keeler line has been variously known in its history as the Carson & Colorado Railroad (named for the two rivers it was intended to connect), the Nevada & California Railway, and finally its last designation in the Southern Pacific camp. The C&C was incorporated under the laws of Nevada on May 19, 1880, and became one of the pioneer narrow-gauge lines in the American West.

The road was projected by Senator William Sharon, Hume Yerington, and Darius Mills, all directors of the famous Virginia & Truckee Railway. Construction commenced at Mound House, just east of Carson City, from a connection with the V&T, whose line connected with the Southern Pacific at Reno. As construction was underway, a number of prosperous mining camps were flourishing — like Bodie, Benton and Candelaria. After the road finally reached Candelaria, the price of silver fell and the board of directors found it inadvisable to build to the Colorado River as planned. The route of the road was diverted instead to Keeler, in the Owens Valley, location of extensive quantities of borax and soda from Owens Lake.

In the gathering twilight of the California desert, old No. 9 of the Southern Pacific narrow-gauge Owens Valley branch, once the famed Carson & Colorado, runs between Oweyno and Keeler. — DONALD DUKE

In passing through to California, by way of Montgomery Pass, the line rose to an elevation of 7,138 feet. For a time this was the highest point on the entire Southern Pacific system. The entire right-of-way from Tonopah Junction (near Candelaria) to Laws was built to avoid tunneling and to keep the maximum compensating grade at three percent. The engineers could not avoid the one tunnel under Mount Montgomery which took the tracks through a 247 foot bore at the summit.

Once the tracks reached Laws, in the upper Owens Valley, the grading and track laying was swift as the crews worked on the east side of the valley to Keeler. Darius Mills, who had never been too enthusiastic over the change in destination to Keeler, made a trip to end-of-track with Sharon and Yerington. As he gazed out over the dun-colored desert wasteland he is said to have remarked: "Gentlemen, it seems to me that either we have built this railroad 300 miles too long or 300 years too soon." In 1900, the Southern Pacific offered to buy the line for $2,750,000 and the sale was completed quickly. Five years later the Goldfield bonanza followed and the Carson & Colorado was to repay the purchase price in one year. The road was so busy the narrow-gauge became an appendage with no physical connection with the main line. The SP made overtures to purchase the Virginia & Truckee, but the asking price was too high. To further its aims the SP early in 1905 formed the Nevada & California Railway into its corporate structure to take over the narrow-gauge and to build a bypass line to avoid giving the V&T any of the traffic from the mines. A 28-mile standard gauge line was constructed between Churchill and Hazen and two rails were laid outside the narrow-gauge rails on the Carson & Colorado between Mound House and Mina until adjustments could be made in the service. While this would leave the narrow-gauge high and dry as a stub from Mina to Keeler it was the most practical solution.

While the Comstock rush was at its height the Cerro Gordo mine, near Owens Lake, produced millions in silver bullion. Despite the decline of the Comstock, the road serviced isolated mining strikes.

In order to handle the construction materials of the Los Angeles Aqueduct the Nevada & California began construction of a standard gauge line from SP's San Joaquin Valley line at Mojave into the Owens Valley in 1908. Called the "Jawbone" line, this road was completed to Owenyo and a connection with the Carson & Colorado narrow-gauge before the Nevada & California merged into the Southern Pacific completely. Over the next 25 years many of the mines played out and more and more of the ore was shipped over the narrow-gauge to the transfer at Owenyo instead of Mina. The line over Montgomery Pass saw little service except during the livestock season and the line between Mina and Laws over Montgomery Pass was abandoned, thus leaving the 70 miles of track between Keeler and Laws isolated except for the connection at Owenyo.

Although the old Carson & Colorado had shrunk from its original 300 miles to 70.5, the pike remained very unique. The freight carried was about the oddest of any railroad, with such products as talc, soda, pumice, clay, soapstone, dolomite, slate, lead, melanterite, and seasonal livestock. Talc accounted for 75 percent of the line's tonnage.

Unlike most narrow-gauge transfer points with a standard gauge line, the junction at Owenyo, 17 miles north of Keeler, had no three-rail trackage. The slim gauge cars were spotted on adjacent tracks to conventional cars, separated only by a platform. Contents that could not be dumped were transferred by conveyor belt. The bulk commodities were run up a ramp that straddled the standard gauge cars and dumped.

Twenty-three different steam locomotives have operated over the whole line and every one, with a single exception, was built by the Baldwin Locomotive Works. The last three active engines before dieselization were Nos. 8, 9 and 18. No. 8 was retired early in 1954 and resides at the Nevada State Museum in Carson City. No. 18 was retired later the same year and given to the city of Independence for display, while No. 9 was kept for emergency service in case the diesel broke down. All three engines saw service on the Nevada-California-Oregon Railway and were inherited when the SP standard gauged the line.

It was remarkable that the Keeler branch remained at all and continued to be profitable enough in the diesel age to warrant keeping the line and acquire an internal combustion engine. For the record the diesel machine was a 45-tonner carried on the roster as No. 1. It was built by General Electric and contained a Caterpillar 450-hp. engine. When the diesel took over as the prime means of motive power, the road had 105 boxcars, 61 gondolas, 39 stock cars, 8 flats, two water cars, a baggage car and caboose. Most of the rolling stock was of 1890 vintage with arch bar trucks.

Like everything else all good things must come to an end. While the diesel did not provide the railroad photographer nice rolling smoke from the stack, it was still the last vestige of common-carrier narrow-gauge in the West. The legend of its great days will live on forever.

The old weathered station at Keeler once dispatched trainloads of silver, lead and zinc, plus a bit of gold, from the famous Cerro Gordo mine north and east of Keeler. Ore was carried to trackside by an aerial tramway system. — DONALD DUKE

The engine repair facilities were located out in the open at Keeler, a spot with Death Valley like weather. In the above scene, No. 18 and its caboose coach takes on water before the trek to Owenyo. (RIGHT) The southern end of the Southern Pacific narrow-gauge was surrounded by desolation. In the hillsides of the Inyo Mountains above its tracks, prospectors found traces of silver, lead, talc and soda dust. Ore was taken out by mule to trackside loading tipples which added a penultimate note of inferno. — BOTH DONALD DUKE

The Owens Valley was virtually 70 miles of flat, unbroken desert surrounded by mountains, but it wasn't all that way or not until Los Angeles bought up all the land and stole the water. The narrow-gauge followed the eastern edge of the Inyo Mountains to be closer to the mines. Between Owenyo, and the end of the line at Keeler, the rails dash across the valley floor with sand between the ties. Just five miles across the valley the land was rich in grass for grazing and California's highest peak — Mount Whitney — reached toward the heavens. In the high desert country the air is so clear you can see smoke miles away. In the above scene, No. 18 makes its way down the valley to Keeler. (OPPOSITE PAGE) The crossing buck at Mt. Whitney siding gave the motorist an upside down warning of No. 18's arrival. (LEFT) Blowing sand collects between the ties as No. 9 polishes the rails. — ALL DONALD DUKE

ROAD
CROSSING
RAI

No. 18 steams down the Owens Valley near Dolomite. She is en route to Keeler to pick up a train load of chemicals from the Natural Soda Products Company, just two miles south of town. — DONALD DUKE

On the return run from Keeler, No. 18 and six loads approach Dolomite, midway between Keeler and Owenyo. In the scene below, No. 18 backs down the spur to gather three loads of talc. Chemicals and talc were the last remaining cargo for the aging narrow-gauge. — BOTH DONALD DUKE

The Los Angeles Acqueduct took five years to build (1908-1913) and cost City of Los Angeles taxpayers $23,000,000 to build. The 223-mile pipeline converted the parched San Fernando Valley of Los Angeles into a rich "market basket," but ruthlessly turned Owens Valley into a semi-desert. The Southern Pacific built a standard gauge line up from Mojave on the main line to haul in supplies for the aqueduct and extended the rails on to Oweyno. Overnight this place became a stopover for crews and transfer point from narrow-to-standard which previously had been shipped over Montgomery Pass to Hawthorne, Nevada. (ABOVE) No. 19 is about to leave Owenyo for Laws, the north end of the line. The Owenyo Hotel is located behind the lumber at the left. — JOHN KRAUSE

Old No. 9 switches a train of talc at Owenyo while the caboose-coach rest alongside the depot. (LEFT) No. 18 backs up the narrow-gauge transfer trestle south of the depot. Here ore and talc were dumped into standard gauge gondolas rolled underneath. (LOWER LEFT) A string of gondolas are being run under the transfer. (BELOW) A brakeman rides a water car in the Oweyno yard. — ALL DONALD DUKE

Rolling along on the slim rails through the sand. With a consist of 15 cars and the caboose-coach on the tail, engineer Bill Ferguson pulls back on the throttle as steam is converted to power. — JOHN KRAUSE

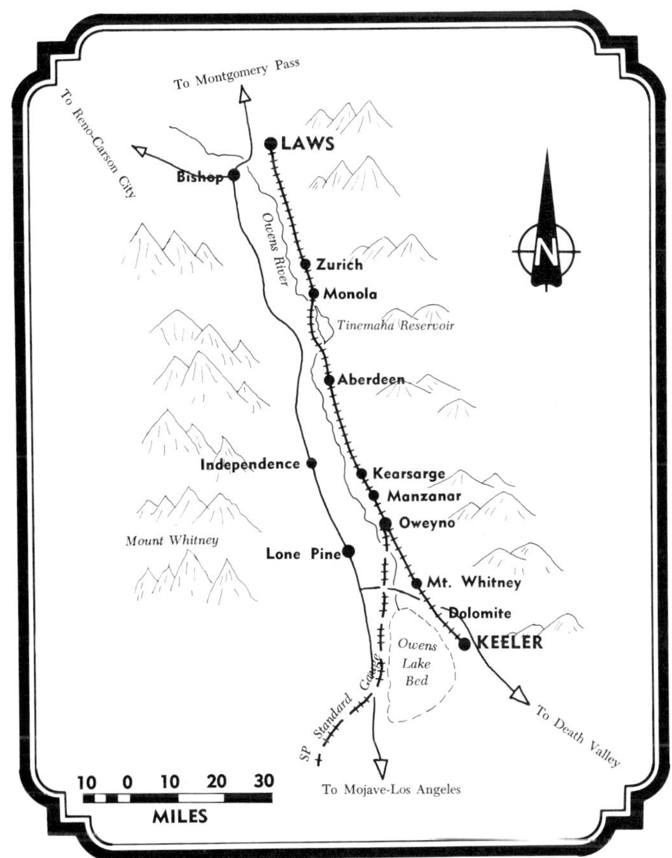

This scene is Kearsarge, a perfect example of how a lush valley can be turned into a desert when water is taken away. Here No. 9 has just taken water and pulls out for Laws. The Kearsarge depot stood for years unused. — DONALD DUKE

Lights and shadows, sage and the high Sierra, as No. 22 rolls down through the grass of Owens Valley between Aberdeen and Kearsarge. No. 22 is a souvenir of the Florence & Cripple Creek and the Nevada-California-Oregon Railway. — DONALD DUKE

22
22

The great Owens Valley runs for 85 miles in a trough. Although little rain falls here, the Owens River received the runoff of the mountains and turned the area around Aberdeen into lush orchards. The trees were destroyed so they would not trap one drop of water destined for parched San Fernando Valley. In the scene above, No. 18 takes on water, then takes off for Kearsarge as may be seen in the view below. — BOTH DONALD DUKE

Rising pillars of oil smoke pile high into the sky as No. 9 and its train roll through Zurich. This spot was always a large shipping point of talc as manifest by the string of gondolas all loaded at the right of this scene. No. 9 will pick these up for transfer on the return run from Laws. (BELOW) A Sierra silhouette of snow and gray granite pinnacles of Mount Whitney dwarf No. 18 as she works along the line north of Laws. — BOTH DONALD DUKE

At Laws, the engineer and fireman turn No. 18 on the hand-operated gallows turntable. (BELOW) No. 18 is shown steaming out of the tree-grown yard at Laws, nothern terminus of the line. At one time Laws was only a water stop tank town on the old Carson & Colorado Railroad, when the railroad ran from the Nevada desert into California via Montgomery Pass. — BOTH DONALD DUKE

Laws station looking south toward Owenyo. The only signals on the branch were the order board station indicators and the telegraph. — DONALD DUKE

The fireman hops onto the tender and pulls down the spout at Laws. (LEFT) Stub switches and harp switchbands were nearly all removed by the 1940's. All that remained was the stubs at Laws as shown below. The track in the center bending to the left leads to the water and oil facility and Keeler. The center track in the distance runs to the gallows turntable, while the other track is a spur which runs off into the grass and comes to an end. — DONALD DUKE

Although it is high desert in the Owens Valley, it still snows there at times. Here No. 8 races the snowstorm blowing off towering Mount Whitney as she steams toward Laws. Strange, with all this ground water around, old No. 8 still must stop at Kearsarge for water. This handsome engine was built by Baldwin in 1907 for the Nevada-California-Oregon. — DONALD DUKE

The water and oil facilities at Laws are the only remaining mementos of the Southern Pacific narrow-gauge today. They are part of the Laws Railroad Museum which includes some cars and a locomotive, plus the depot. In the above scene, No. 8 takes on water. The station can be seen in the background. (RIGHT) No. 8 and its train crossing the Owens River bridge. — BOTH DONALD DUKE

Twenty-three different steam locomotives have operated over the slim rails since they were laid and every one, with a single exception, was built by the Baldwin Locomotive Works. As parts became hard to come by the Southern Pacific considered either abandonment of the branch or buying a diesel. Since it might take time to close the line, a 45-ton 450 hp. diesel was ordered from the General Electric Company that had special trucks which could be used on narrow-gauge or standard. The No. 1 with its Caterpillar engine arrived during October 1954 and was officially welcomed with special ceremonies held by the Southern California Chapter — RAILWAY & LOCOMOTIVES HISTORICAL SOCIETY. (ABOVE) A Southern Pacific official giving an address in front of the Owenyo Hotel. (BELOW) No. 1 as she looked in service just outside the Owenyo depot. — BOTH DONALD DUKE

Walter Thrall, chairman of the Southern California Chapter — Railway & Locomotive Historical Society has just christened No. 1 with a bottle of homegrown talc. He holds up the locomotives official name *Little Giant*. The diesel was the prime power on the line until the last official run on April 29, 1960. This brought to a close 80 years of narrow-gauge operation. Diesel No. 1 was too light for most standard gauge chores on the Southern Pacific, so she was sold during April 1961 to the Pan American Engineering Company. — DONALD DUKE

The West Side rails bend around 'em. A piece of tangent track was the exception rather than the rule. Here, No. 8 with a string of empty flats. — DONALD DUKE

7

West Side Lumber

California's West Side Lumber Company's logging railroad was nearly overlooked by iron horse historians until it was discovered this was the last narrow-gauge logger in the American West and custodian of the largest stable of steam locomotives running within the state. When they did descend with camera and tape recorder upon the secluded tracks that wound high out of the Sierra foothills at Tuolumne, they were almost too late. By 1960, the curious, sidewinder Shay geared locomotives had ceased their ratchety echoing among the sugar pine.

The logging road began life in 1900 as the Hetch Hetchy & Yosemite Valley Railway. The line had great hopes of engaging in the profitable passenger hauls into the spectacular glacial canyons of Yosemite, Hetch Hetchy, and over to neighboring Calaveras Big Trees. Like so many railroads whose names bespoke greater intent than their accomplishments, this road never reached these scenic centers.

The West Side relegated its three-foot rails to the hauling of logs. At one time its rails reached 70 miles into the high Sierra Country — almost to the corner of today's Yosemite National Park. Add to this some 250 miles of logging spurs that had been laid (and torn up as the timber was logged off) and you have quite an operation. Also consider that the main line of the road never reached beyond an 18-mile line as the crow would fly eastward from its starting point — a remarkable concentration of railroading winding around the canyons and valleys.

The West Side handled its chores with little fanfare through World War II times. While logging pikes were becoming something on the order of collectors' items, the West Side even as late as 1958 presented to everyone a picture of health. All of a sudden the mill was sold to the Pickering Lumber Co. of Kansas City whose board had other ideas about narrow-gauge. The railroad was finished.

The West Side was famous for its steam roster which consisted mainly of Shay geared locomotives built by the Lima Locomotives Works, four Heislers, several saddle tankers, a Plymouth diesel to work the mill, and several standard gauge locomotives to work the exchange tracks.

For all the dreamers' disappointments, the West Side was a lot of narrow-gauge railroad and a pleasure to watch and photograph while it was alive.

The engineer checks over the gears on his Shay before taking off for Buffalo Landing, the last operating railhead on the line. — DONALD DUKE (RIGHT) Shay No. 9 leaves Tuolumne for the woods with a tanker of fuel for the woods equipment and a string of flats. The brakeman often rode the tender and was protected from the sun by an umbrella. — JOHN KRAUSE

Blowing like a blowtorch, Shay No. 8 rolls through Bakers Siding en route to Camp 8. In this scene her vertical rods are pumping in a shower of water and lubrication. — JOHN KRAUSE

Steel rails curving high across rivers on wood bridges that stand 50 to 75 feet above the water are a good substitute for solid ground. West Side had four big trestles spanning ravines. In this scene, No. 8 clatters across River Bridge crossing the North Fork of the Tuolumne River. — DONALD DUKE

The serpentine trackage below Straight Siding slowed log trains down to a crawl. (BELOW) The majority of West Side's cabooses were homemade products, but handled the job. — BOTH DONALD DUKE (RIGHT) No. 10 has just crossed river bridge and charges upgrade to Mustang and then drops down into Tuolumne. — JOHN KRAUSE

The River Bridge was unique because of a straight section in the center with curved approaches on each end. Late one afternoon No. 10 and her train made a crossing with a tonnage train of fir and pine logs. Photographer Krause was on hand to capture the scene on film.

8

Sumpter Valley

The prime power on the Sumpter Valley was a pair of monstrous mallet locomotives originally designed for service on the Uintah Railway, and here, near McEwen on of them is working eastbound with 30 cars of finished lumber. — LUCIUS BEEBE

Oregon's most notable and one of the longest lived of all the narrow-gauge railways of the Pacific Northwest, was built in the great days of the lumber barons in the Blue Mountains where vast stands of virgin timber covered every slope, mountain and valley. The hungry humming saws of the mills were the motivating force behind the Sumpter Valley. Locomotives shifted logs from hillside to millpond, and then hauled the finished lumber to the Union Pacific at Baker. This was an age when three-foot tracks were popular, with freight and daily passenger trains listed on the time table. The completion of highways and the decline of lumbering in its region spelled the slow death for this railroad of happy memories.

Born along with the SV were an array of private logging railroads which snaked out long trains of logs with such geared power as Shays, Climaxes and Heislers.

With the inauguration of train service in 1896, there came a gold bonanza. Though short lived, it enriched the treasury and added color to its history. Soon after the turn-of-the-century, cattlemen discovered the lush grass along the Sumpter and dispatched prime beef to Portland's packing houses.

This 60 mile line was unique in contemporary railroading due to its array of secondhand locomotives and rolling stock. Most famous motive power were its two 2-6-6-2 Mallets originally designed for the Uintah Railway and the only narrow-gauge locomotives of their kind in the U.S. Until the thirties most of the road's

locomotives still used wood for fuel!

The railroad became a gathering place for secondhand rolling stock. Flats, log cars, boxcars and tanks came from such legendary lines as Denver, South Park & Pacific, Colorado Central, Carson & Colorado, and the fabled Rio Grande Southern. The roster was a virtual potpourri of every known make and variety of narrow-gauge equipment.

A bright summer day in 1946 marked the final steam main line run of the Sumpter Valley. A 1.5 mile dual gauge switching line remained until December 27, 1961, along with the Oregon Lumber Company mill.

Presented here are the last good days of the narrow-gauge Sumpter Valley Railway.

The aromatic pungency of wood smoke, hot metal and valve oil fills the Oregon countryside near Salisbury, as No. 16 rolls a westbound train of empty lumber flats. — HENRY R. GRIFFITHS, JR.

The road had a variety of wooden boxcars and No. 1351 is typical of the road's equipment. Note the wood bolster arch bar trucks on this car. (BELOW) Located 16 miles west of Baker, Oregon, Boulder Gorge was the most scenic spot on the railroad. Here the line crossed the Powder River on *Red Bridge* due to its early red boxcar color. — BOTH HENRY R. GRIFFITHS, JR.

The U. S. Gypsum's motive power in 1946 consisted of No. 12 a Porter 2-6-0, No. 8 a Baldwin 2-8-0, and a Whitcomb diesel complete with rods carry its original U. S. Government number of 40. During 1952 it was necessary to scrap No. 12 and No. 8 was due for an overhaul. The road found itself short of power, so it called on the Southern Pacific for help. They sent down No. 9 from Owenyo and it saw three weeks service during the summer. In the above scene, No. 9 is about the leave the processor at Plaster City for the mine 27 miles distant at Fish Creek. — RICHARD STEINHEIMER

9

U.S. Gypsum

The 26-mile pike of the U.S. Gypsum Company, located in the extreme southern corner of California along the Mexican border, is the state's last industrial narrow-gauge. The General Electric 400 hp. multiple unit diesels back-to-back make two round trips daily with empties and loads to and from the gypsum mine at Fish Creek.

While searching for oil in the western section of the Imperial Valley in 1906, a survey team came upon a mountain with outcroppings of a white material. After tests it was found the entire mountain contained a large deposit of gypsum. The Imperial Valley Gypsum & Oil Corporation was established to mine and market the ore, but it remained impractical until the San Diego & Arizona Railroad was built in 1921 connecting San Diego with El Centro.

A survey from the railroad at Dunaway City began in April 1921, and progressed out over the sandy waste to the gypsum mountain. A narrow gauge road was built and the final spike driven in late September 1922.

The road began operations with a former Colusa & Lake Railway 4-4-0 and 10-ore cars running on 35-pound rails. In one year the firm became California's largest gypsum producer, but lacked sufficient capital to expand the physical plant. The Imperial Company sold out to the Pacific Portland Cement Company in 1924, who in turn purchased two 2-6-0's from the Arizona & New Mexico Railway to handle the volume. During 1936 a Plymouth 0-4-0 gasoline switcher was added and a former Nevada County Narrow-Gauge Railway 2-8-0 during World War II.

After 22 years of ownership, the holdings were sold to the United States Gypsum Company in 1946. Long range plans included complete upgrading of the railroad and physical plant. The rail was converted from 35-pound iron to new 70-pound steel. A secondhand Navy 300 hp. Whitcomb was obtained in 1946 and a new 600 hp. Porter was delivered in 1949.

Further improvements made in the mid-fifties included two General Electric 50-ton engines, an automatic unloader at the processor and a new loading facility at Fish Creek.

Today the narrow-gauge is a very effective industrial line. Ninety pound rail is in place, a fleet of new 50-ton air operated dump cars with roller bearing trucks and a capacity to handle 1,000 tons of gypsum in two scheduled round trip runs per day with 20 cars. With an annual production of over 500,000 tons of gypsum products including wallboard, rock lath, and casting or ceramic plasters, the firm has now exceeded the visions of its original builders.

The Whitcomb diesel worked the yard at Plaster City switching cars. She was just too light to bring in the tonnage of ore for the processor. In the above scene, she shoves empties to No. 9 waiting for another run to Fish Creek. (LEFT) The fireman checks his air pressure gauge as his tanks fill the train line. — BOTH DICK STEINHEIMER

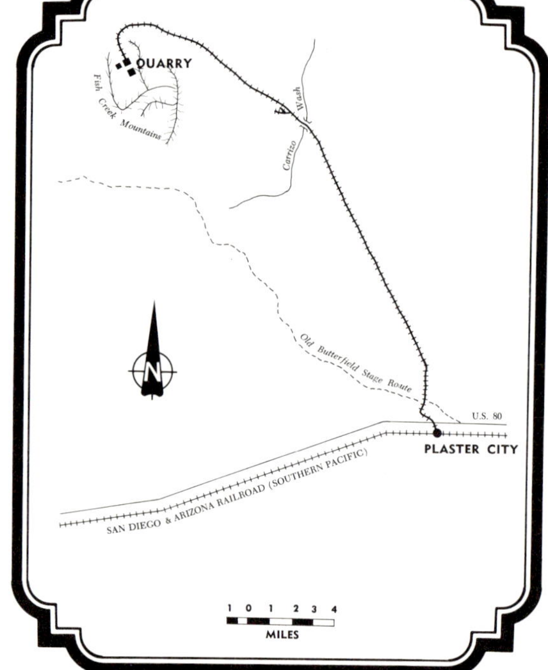

The brakeman waits for the familiar "Highball" so he can throw the switch after the train passes. — DICK STEINHEIMER

In 1949 a 600 hp. Porter diesel was acquired and assisted No. 1203. In the above scene the new machine leaves the mine at Fish Creek for Plaster City. The strange car behind the diesel is a homemade steel caboose with employee compartment in the center and flat car space at each end used to haul supplies to the mine. — DONALD DUKE (RIGHT) One of two General Electric diesels Nos. 1303 and 1403 which has backed a string of hoppers into the underground loader. The engine then moves slowly forward as the cars are filled. (BELOW) Rolling a train of empties back to the mine, a pair of GE's back-to-back roll across one of the many trestles on the 27-mile line. — BOTH DENIS DUNNING

At Skagway, the main line of the White Pass & Yukon rolled down the town's main street, imaginatively named Broadway. During wartime the line was so busy the trackage was moved behind the buildings at the left. — YUKON ARCHIVES

10

White Pass & Yukon

America's last remaining common carrier three-foot line is the White Pass & Yukon Route, running between Skagway, Alaska, and the headwaters of the Yukon River at Whitehorse, Canada, a distance of 110 miles.

The railroad owes its existence to a gold strike along Bonanza Creek in Canada's Yukon Territory in 1896 and it reached its climax by 1898. This "gold fever" sent thousands of prospectors into the region by way of Skagway — the shortest distance from the ocean to the gold country. Overnight a town of shacks became a settlement and supply center of 15,000 as fortune seekers came by ship from Seattle and Pacific Points.

The demand for transportation was so great it gave impetus to a plan to build a narrow-gauge railway from Skagway, over White Pass, to Bennett in British Columbia, then on into the Yukon. To accomplish this three separate companies — the Pacific & Arctic Railway & Navigation Co. (in Alaska), the British Columbia Yukon Railway (in British Columbia) and the British Yukon Mining, Trading & Transportation Co. (in Yukon Territory) were formed. Together, these three carriers were to be a continuous rail link from Skagway to Fort Selkirk on the Yukon, a rail distance of 325 miles. The line was surveyed in 1898 and a portion in Alaska placed in operation the same year.

A few days after the first run, on July 20, 1898 to be exact, the charter rights of the three roads became the White Pass & Yukon Railway Company Ltd. Construction continued at a rapid pace and reached White Pass, at an elevation of 2,885 feet, 20 miles from Skagway by February 1899, and on July 9 it reached Bennett, at the head of the lake of the same name. The portion included a 250 foot tunnel, the 215 foot high Dead Horse viaduct, grades of 3.9 percent and 20 degree curves. During the summer construction was moving southward from White Horse, and on July 29, 1900 the two sections joined at Caribou Crossing (Carcross). Two weeks later regular service was inaugurated along with steamers on the Yukon River between Whitehorse and Dawson, 434 miles.

During World War II the U.S. Army operated the road which hauled supplies for building the Alcan Highway. Narrow-gauge steam locomotives from all over America were secured and pressed into service.

The White Pass Route still operates over its initial 110 miles of route opened in 1900, and it is still narrow-gauge. Today the road is quite modern having heavy rail, a fleet of diesel locomotives and handling containers all the way from Vancouver in its own vessels.

The ocean-rail terminal at Skagway is the heart of the White Pass & Yukon line. Here at the headwaters of the Lynn Canal, the high mountains rise from the waters edge and form a natural harbor. — YUKON ARCHIVES (LEFT) In the battle to the summit of the line, a steel cantilever bridge spectacularly spans Dead Horse Gulch 215 feet above the rushing waters below. — R. P. MIDDLEBROOK (BELOW) The 111.7-mile narrow-gauge is rich in memories of the Klondike gold rush, complete with open platform wooden coaches. At Bennett, the vintage era train is flanked by the station and restaurant. — CANADIAN PACIFIC

This two engine mixed train, headed by a former wartime U. S. Army 2-8-2, is assisted by White Pass No. 69 a 2-8-0, and is shown here clattering across the Dead Horse Gulch viaduct. Construction of this viaduct was slowed down by news of gold strikes in Alaska and the Yukon. Workmen left their jobs to join in with the prospectors. Before the steel bridge was completed, the WP&Y made use of a switchback up the gulch. — CANADIAN PACIFIC

A pair of General Electric "cab" engines wait patiently at Whitehorse station for an eastbound ore extra powered by new Montreal Locomotive Works DL 530's to clear the main line. — THE STUDIO

The splendor of winter, narrow-gauge railroading modern container transport, and Dead Horse Gulch viaduct all blend together in this spectacular White Pass & Yukon scene. — THE STUDIO

Against the background of the imposing Alaskan countryside, a pair of Montreal Locomotive Works DL 530's sand the wet rails as they leave Carcross in Yukon Territory. The unusual tub-like containers carry lead and zinc concentrates from a mine in the territory to Skagway for trans-shipment. — THE STUDIO

The Kahului Railroad was short in mileage, but spectacular in the bridge department. In this scene, No. 12 clatters across Kuiaha Gulch on a latticework wooden trestle, 330 feet long and 130 feet above the ravine. — MURRAY BEFELER

11

Hawaiian Railroads

Narrow-gauge railroading got started in the Hawaiian Islands shortly after the slim rails began to scale Colorado's Rocky Mountains. In Colorado the urge to extend rails stemmed from the wealth of mines; in Hawaii the yield was sugar.

The epidemic of railroad building in the Islands gained impetus with the ratification of the reciprocal trade treaty by the U.S. Congress in 1876 which permitted Hawaiian raw sugar entry into the U.S. without duty. With the expansion of the sugar industry, railroads began to grow after King Kalakaua signed an act "To Promote the Construction of Railways," in 1878.

The immediate result was the building of the first line, the Kahului & Wailuku Railroad, between the two named Maui towns. Train service began on July 20, 1879, initiating the first common carrier railroad in the islands. The direct descendent of this pioneer line was the 16-mile Kahului Railroad. Although other narrow-gauge railroads blossomed on other islands, this pioneer road outlasted them all. It was not abandoned until 1967, providing nearly 88 years of service.

By far the largest slim gauge operation was the Oahu Railway & Land Company on the island of Oahu, the seat of the Hawaiian Government. The road was organized in 1888 by Benjamin Dillingham, who planned to encircle the entire island with rails, but never constructed track beyond the village of Kahuku, a distance of 71.3 miles from Honolulu.

The first regularly scheduled passenger train out of Honolulu left the city on King Kalakaua's birthday, November 16, 1889, and in time 172 miles of track were spiked down on the island. The topography of Oahu governed the railroad's route and was why engineers built the main line to hug the coastline.

Out of Honolulu the railroad was double tracked to Waipahu, 14 miles distant, junction point for the branch to Schofield Barracks. While the main line contained little grade, the Wahiawa branch climbed from sea level up Waikakalaua Gulch, on a three percent grade, to a thousand-foot plateau in 10 miles.

In early days the freight traffic was light, but with increased sugar output and the success of James D. Dole in growing pineapples, things picked up. For years the train was the only means of public transportation around the island.

The OR&L is probably the only American narrow-gauge to have had block signals on its double track and was the first railroad in the world to use telephone train dispatching.

The road's finest hour followed December 7, 1941, when the road broke all freight and passenger traffic records. But the inevitable was in the offing following World War II. The entire system, save the Honolulu terminal area, was abandoned as of December 31, 1947 and the entire line closed by 1972.

Rolling through the cane fields on the north shore of Maui isthmus. (BELOW) No. 12 switches Pier 2 at Kakului Harbor. The piers have warehouse capacity for storing large quantities of freight and canned pineapples. Adjacent is a bulk sugar plant with space for 26,000 tons of raw sugar delivered from the mills by rail. — BOTH MURRAY BEFELER

A trainload of pineapples off the Wahiawa branch of the Oahu Railway & Land Company line winds through the junction tracks at Waipahu and heads eastward along the outskirts of Pearl Harbor en route to the Honolulu docks. — KENT W. COCHRANE

The rocky, cactus-covered walls of Waikakalua Creek echo to the screech of brakes as this Wahiawa branch way freight clears the distant signal board as it approaches close to Wahiawa junction. Once through the junction, the train will skirt Pearl Harbor en route to the Honolulu docks. — KENT W. COCHRANE

At the conclusion of World War II naval personnel returning home were cleared through Pearl Harbor leaving sailors with spare time on their hands. The Oahu Railway solved this dilemma by running excursions to Barber's Point. In the scene at the right, No. 85 under a rolling cloud of smoke clears the Honolulu yard with a train of sailors for the Point. (CENTER) No. 90 heads south near Kaena Point on the north side of the Island of Oahu. (BELOW) A long freight steams along the surf between Waialua and Kaena Point. — ALL KENT W. COCKRANE

West Coast Industrials

Teledyne Potash

In the shadow of Carlsbad Caverns National Park in the southeastern corner of New Mexico, ran Teledyne Potash Company's three-foot gauge industrial line. The railroad ran from the mill near Loving to a quarry 18 miles distant. The road was operated by two 70-ton General Electric diesels which could easily handle a train of 30 loaded hoppers. When the supply of potash ran out in 1972, the road was abandoned. — GARY ALLEN

Monolith Portland Cement

A Southern California narrow-gauge industrial recently abandoned was Monolith Portland Cement's three-mile line near Tehachapi that hauled ore from a hillside to the mill. The railroad included two 40-ton Plymouth locomotives and 40 ore cars. Only one engine was in service at a time. The operation consisted of the engine picking up 16 ore cars, a run to the mine, loading through a dumper, and a return trip to a rotary dumper at the plant. — BOTH GARY ALLEN

Bibliography

Books

Anderson, George L. *Kansas West,* San Marino: Golden West Books, 1963.

Athearn, Robert. *The Denver and Rio Grande Western Railroad,* Lincoln: University of Nebraska Press, 1962.

Beebe, Lucius. *Mixed Train Daily,* Berkeley: Howell-North Books, 1961.

Beebe, Lucius. *The Narrow Gage Railroads of Colorado,* Boston: The Railway & Locomotive Historical Society, 1946.

Beebe, Lucius and Clegg, Charles. *Narrow Gauge in the Rockies,* Berkeley: Howell-North Books, 1958.

Beebe, Lucius and Clegg, Charles. *Rio Grande Mainline of the Rockies,* Berkeley: Howell-North Books, 1963.

Best, Gerald M. *Railroads of Hawaii,* San Marino: Golden West Books, 1978.

Best, Gerald M. *Ulster & Delaware,* San Marino: Golden West Books, 1972.

Bowles, Samuel. *The War of the Gauges,* Colorado Springs: Western Books, 1871.

Bruce, Alfred W. *The Steam Locomotive in America,* New York: W. W. Norton & Co., Inc., 1952.

Choda, Kelly. *Thirty Pound Rails,* Aurora: The Filter Press, 1956.

Crum, Josie Moore. *The Rio Grande Southern Story,* Durango: Railroadiana, Inc. Publishers, 1957.

Davis, E. O. *The First Five Years of the Railroad Era in Colorado,* Golden: Sage Books, Inc., 1948.

Davis, J.T. *Narrow Gauge Railroads,* San Francisco: George Spaulding & Co., 1880.

Duke, Donald. *Southern Pacific Steam Locomotives,* San Marino: Golden West Books, 1955.

Ellis, Erl H. *A Broad Gauge Tail on a Narrow-Gauge Dog,* Brand Book 10: Westerners-Denver Posse, 1954.

Ferrell, Mallory Hope. *Rails, Sagebrush & Pine,* San Marino: Golden West Books, 1967.

Ferrell, Mallory Hope. *Silver San Juan - The Rio Grande Southern Railroad,* Boulder: Pruett Publishing, 1973.

Ferrell, Mallory Hope. *Tweetsie Country,* Boulder: Pruett Publishing Co., 1976.

Fisher, John. *A Builder of the West,* Caldwell: The Caxton Printers, Ltd., 1939.

Fleming, Howard. *Narrow Gauge Railway in America,* Lancaster: Inquirer Printing & Publishing Co., 1875.

Fleming, Howard. *Narrow Gauge Railway in America,* Lancaster: Inquirer Printing & Publishing Co., (Second Edition), 1876.

Forney, Matthias N. *The Car-Builder's Dictionary,* New York: The Railroad Gazette, 1879.

Hungerford, John B. *Hawaiian Railroads,* Reseda: Hungerford Press, 1963.

Hungerford, John B. *The Slim Princess,* Reseda: Hungerford Press, 1956.

Kramer, Frederick A. *Twilight on the Narrow Gauge,* New York: Quadrant Press, Inc., 1976.

Krause, John. *Rails Through Dixie,* San Marino: Golden West Books, 1965.

Krieg, Allan. *Last of the 3-Foot Loggers,* San Marino: Golden West Books, 1962.

Kyper, Frank. *A Ramble Into The Past on The East Broad Top Railroad,* Rockhill Furnace: East Broad Top Railroad and Coal Co., 1971.

Lavalee, Omer. *Narrow Gauge Railways of Canada,* Montreal: Railfare Enterprise, Ltd., 1972.

LeMassena, R.A. *Colorado's Mountain Country Railroads,* Golden: The Smoking Stack Press, 1965.

LeMassena, Robert A. *Rio Grande . . . to The Pacific!,* Denver: Sundance, Ltd., 1974.

Lucas, Walter A. *100 Years of Railroad Cars,* New York: Simmons-Boardman Publishing Co., 1958.

Mannix, Joseph A. *A Quick Review of the East Broad Top,* Bethlehem: ABC Printing, 1960.

Martin, Cy. *Gold Rush Narrow Gauge,* Los Angeles: Trans-Anglo Books, 1971.

McCoy, Dell and Collman, Russ. *The Rio Grande Pictorial,* Denver: Sundance, Ltd., 1971.

Mencken, August. *The Railroad Passenger Car,* Baltimore: The Johns Hopkins Press, 1957.

Myrick, David F. *Railroads of Nevada and Eastern California - Volume One,* Berkeley: Howell-North Books, 1962.

Myrick, David F. *Railroads of Nevada and Eastern California - Volume Two,* Berkeley: Howell-North Books, 1963.

Reid, H. *Extra South,* Morristown: Compton Press, Inc., 1964.

Scheer, Julian and Mc D. Black, Elizabeth. *Tweetsie, The Blue Ridge Stemwinder,* Charlotte: Heritage House, 1958.

Spooner, C.E. *Narrow Gauge Railways,* London: William Clowes & Son, 1871.

Steinheimer, Richard. *Backwoods Railroads of the West,* Milwaukee: Kalmbach Publishing Company, 1963.

Stover, John F. *American Railroads,* Chicago: University of Chicago Press, 1961.

Talbot, Fred A. *Cassell's Railways of the World,* New York: Simmons-Boardman Publishing Co., 1925.

Thode, Jackson C. *A Century of Passenger Trains: A Study of 100 Years of Service on the Denver & Rio Grande Railway, Its Heirs, Successors and Assigns,* Brand Book 26: Westerners-Denver Posse, 1971.

Turner, George. *Narrow Gauge Nostalgia,* Harbor City: J-H Publications, 1965.

Turner, George. *Slim Rails Through the Sand,* Long Beach: Johnston & Howe, 1963.

Vauclain, Samuel. *History of the Baldwin Locomotive Works, 1831-1923,* Philadelphia: Baldwin Locomotive Works, 1924.

Wheeler, Keith. *The Railroaders,* New York: Time-Life Books, 1973.

White, John H. Jr. *The American Railroad Passenger Car,* Baltimore: The Johns Hopkins University Press, 1978.

Whitehouse, P.B. and Allen, P.C. *Round the World on the Narrow Gauge,* London: Ian Allen, Ltd., 1966.

Periodicals

Alexander, Jack. "Tweetsie's Last Trip." *Trains,* Volume 11, No. 3 (January 1951), pp. 24-35.

Athearn, Robert G. "The Denver & Rio Grande Railway." *Colorado Magazine,* Volume 35, No. 1 (April 1958) pp. 1-34.

Beebe, Lucius. "Southern Pacific Narrow Gauge." *Trains,* Volume 7, No. 5 (March 1947), pp. 14-21.

Chappell, Gordon. "Farewell to Cumbres." *Colorado Rail Annual,* Volume 1 (1967), pp. 1-32.

Chappell, Gordon. "Narrow-Gauge Trancontinental I." *Colorado Rail Annual,* Issue No. 8 (1970), pp. 1-99.

Graves, P.C. "The Gold Rush Route." *Railroad Magazine,* Volume 67, No. 3 (April 1956), pp. 48-53.

Hauck, Cornelius W. "Narrow Gauge Trancontinental II." *Colorado Rail Annual,* Issue No. 8 (1970), pp. 100-131.

Hubbard, Freeman. "S.P. Narrow Gage." *Railroad Magazine,* Volume 70, No. 2 (February 1959), pp. 26-29.

Jacques, F. L. "Gateway to the Yukon." *Trains,* Volume 11, No. 3 (January 1951), pp. 36-43.

Krause, John. "Orbisonia Obsession." *Railfan,* Volume 1, No. 5 (Winter 1975), pp. 18-27.

Lenton, David. "East Broad Top Railroad." *Railroad Magazine,* Volume 55, No. 2 (July 1951), pp. 46-55.

Mayer, Harold M. "Main Line of Narrow Gauge." *Trains,* Volume 4, No. 11 (September 1944), pp. 18-25.

Moedinger, William Jr. "Silver San Juan Scenic Line." *Trains,* Volume 2, No. 4 (February 1942), pp. 8-25.

Moore, William C. "White Pass & Yukon." *Trains,* Volume 2, No. 11 (September 1942), pp. 35-41.

Moran, Miles. "Misadventures Under the Sea."

Rail Classics, Volume 5, No. 3 (May 1976), pp. 45-55.

Morgan, David P. "Trains Goes to Alaska - 1." *Trains,* Volume 23, No. 4 (February 1963), pp. 19-25.

Morgan, David P. "Trains Goes to Alaska - 2." *Trains,* Volume 23, No. 5 (March 1963), pp. 30-35.

Osborn, James D. "He Built Narrow-Gage Roads." *Railroad Magazine,* Volume 29, No. 3 (February 1941), pp. 76-85.

Palmer, William J. *Annual Report - Denver & Rio Grande Railway.* Denver, April 1873.

Railroad Gazette. New York, Volumes 5-30 (1873-1898).

Railway & Locomotive Engineering. New York, Volumes 8-16 (1895-1903).

Railway Review. Chicago, Volumes 6-14 (1873-1901).

Rhine, Stan. "Tin Feathers and Gasoline Fumes." *Colorado Rail Annual,* Issue No. 9 (1971), pp. 1-49.

Richardson, Robert W. *Iron Horse News.* Golden, Volumes 1-92 (August 1958 - November 1976).

Richardson, Robert W. *Narrow Gauge News.* Alamosa, Volumes 1-80 (June 1949-July 1958).

Richardson, Robert W. "Rio Grande Southern Calls It Quits." *Trains,* Volume 12, No. 8 (June 1952), pp. 14-15.

Scott, Jeff. "Mining in Three Foot Gauge." *Railroad Modeler,* Volume 3, No. 2 (February 1973), pp. 49-53.

Sloan, Robert E. "The First Denver & Rio Freight Cars 1871-1872." *Narrow Gauge and Short Line Gazette,* Volume 1, No. 2 (May 1975), pp. 12-19.

Steinhilber, Walter. "Dirge for The RGS." *Railroad Magazine,* Volume 60, No. 2 (March 1953), pp. 67-79.

Warner, Paul. "Motive Power Development of the Denver & Rio Grande Western." *Baldwin Locomotives,* Volume 6, No. 3 (January 1928), pp. 3-28; Volume 6, No. 4 (April 1928), pp. 27-44.

Wood, Don. "The Great East Broad Top Revival." *Trains,* Volume 21, No. 2 (December 1960), pp. 26-31.

Kerosene marker lamps on the Ely-Thomas Lumber Company caboose are put in place as the tiny three-foot gauge Shay geared locomotive couples-up for a night run. The white shaft from the headlight uncovers the heavy growth of the West Virginia forest.
— R. J. COOK

Index